WARREN HEAD AND CHRISTCHURCH HAVEN

Lawrence Popplewell

Popplewell, Lawrence

Warren Head and Christchurch Haven -
(Poole Bay Series)

I. Title   II. Series

942.339

British Library Cataloguing in Publication Data

MELLEDGEN PRESS, SOUTHBOURNE, BOURNEMOUTH

ISBN 0 906637-23-6

CONTENTS

INTRODUCTION.

CHRISTCHURCH The Quay. R. Stour.

Christchurch. Meeting of R. Avon & R. Stour.

INTRODUCTION

This little book, my third on this district, seeks now to bring together a collection of information, gathered over the years, which may be of interest to the general reader. It is surprising often, how quickly dates and events get mixed up in the mind, even of those who have lived directly through them and so it is hoped the chronological date sequences and diaries set out here, of all the main attractions around this magical harbour, will help a little to fix time and place and perhaps, jog a few more memories. That way new lines of enquiry may be found and most of all about the area of Warren and Christchurch Harbour - stretching in the west to Tuckton Bridge and Southbourne - such later newness just plonked down on this remnant of tawny antiquity which, with its Reindeer hunters' camp of pre-history serves as a starting point. Thus their hilltop was and is a key place for us locally, even as the land and seascape below has changed so much, past visions here perhaps - and not the vantage point - being most of all, the central difference .

But this text is mainly concerned with how the present seeable world came to be and,

Wick Ferry, Christchurch

by presenting a little more perspective, to help informed debate for the future; new vistas, once again. For the Iron Age era, and the newly discovered and so important Roman one, however, when the Head was guardian to that most important British port - readers may look best to the specialist texts (See Bibliography). For the later devastating ironstone extractions 1848+, though touched on in the Erosion Diary, they may see my Ironstone Canyon, 1986 and, for the true feel of the river community; The Last Village on the Dorset Stour, 1978. This also covers the period post 1970 which, in general, has been the stop date of its fullest discussion.

So here's a little record, a cornucopia of facts about the ancient promontory and riverside which, hopefully, argue and most of all, their own strong case for continued safe protection plus careful improvement of all the remaining wild country and much of the built environment nearby. In sum, it's still a beautiful and dramatic place but, just here and there, the shadows are lengthening.

Lawrence Popplewell
Blackberry Point.
5.xi.92

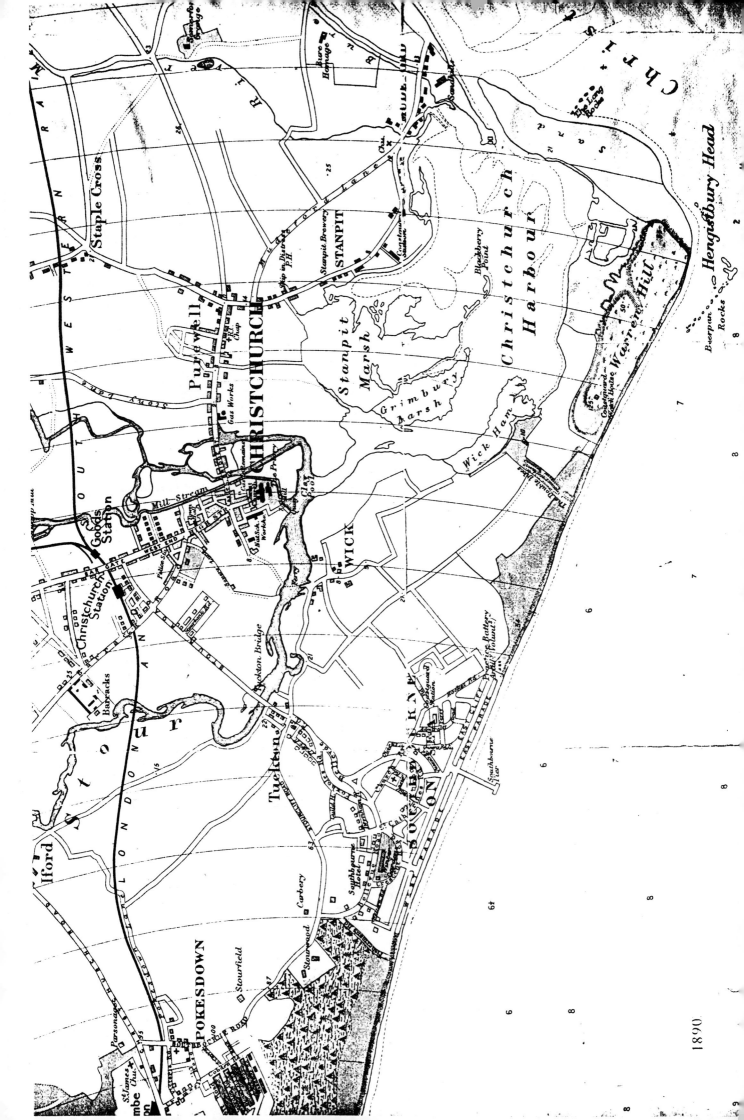

1

INVASION

In the time of Charles II, the French thought to invade England and the King "got Sir Godfrey Flood to make enquiry and draw up a plan of defence for the places where the enemy might deem it possible to land near Christchurch."

State Paper Domestic Ch.11, Vol. 164, No. 70 (AD 1666) "A note on such places as are thought to be considered if the French should attempt to land near the town of Christchurch - by the seamen of those parts."

LOWLANDS   At a place called Lowlands near Christchurch, the channell is such that ships of 150-200 tons may ride safe upon all winds without danger unless the winds blow very hard from the South-West and being a low place they may ride within musquet shot of the shore and by the space of a mile thereabouts the landing place is easy.

HYNESBURY   There is a place called Hynesbury within a mile (of Christchurch) - well known to be a very stronghold entrenched on the land side and compassed upon the other by the sea. This place is thought sufficient for 20,000 men to encamp and live or even many more, and could, if the enemy should take and plant great ordnance there, be such that no man could come near by two miles or better, by sea or land.

For the guard of this place, there is appointed as yet but one company under the leading of William Barrow who has 100 men.

Note: River Avon Navigation Act (1664), the name Hengistbury seems to be an Antiquarian construct dating from the early 17thC and not a geographical term or with any historical connection to Hengist. Even in the course of the 19thC, Christchurch or Warren Head seems to have been at least equally preferred. Whilst, before that, Heddin's Fort is recorded. Interestingly, the first mention of Bournemouth is as La Bournemowthe in the cartulary of Christchurch Priory 1407 and second on a 1539 map. It is noted too as a potential Spanish landing place in a list of 1574 whilst, in the time of Henry VIII, it was seen there "ys feyer landyng" here. Other old local names - along the Western Shore and all close together were Mount Misery, Seven Firs, Kembers Drouk, Acre Ditchmay, Cripple Hedge and Stafford's Cellars. Stanpit was Stony Pit.

These may be a combination of fishermen's and smuggling terms but are all now defunct, as has Warren (Ancient Rabbit preserve) continued to become, if mainly this century.

The Warren here of course, as with Purbeck, probably dated from the early post Norman era; their introduced sun loving Coney, always a reluctant burrower, having to be coddled into establishing itself and usually by means of dry artificial earth pillow mounds (sometimes called Buries, hence ? Hednesburia). Hence Warreners were still making these up until the 19thC although, in the Head's case, they may have just made use of its steeply sloping sides and no doubt, of some of the scattered tumuli 'conveniently' to hand. Certainly it was all a worthwhile enterprise, for rabbit meat, for centuries, was well beyond the reach of the poor and the Warrens mainly exclusive to the Church and Aristocracy - the Warreners leasing the ground at a high rent. On dry infertile heathland also, the pelts (used widely for hat making) would have proved much more profitable than any crops and on the Headland here would be relatively easily protectable against the efficient poaching gangs - these ruthlessly and determinedly active from the 15thC. No doubt too these comprised some of the poor for whom the turning of the skins gave legitimate employment otherwise. We should remember that to poach a rabbit was once a hanging crime in what was, for centuries, a large and profitable industry.

By 1880 however, things had relaxed somewhat, the occupiers of land having permission, by Act of Parliament, to take rabbits found on their land. As the escapees from Warrens became more and more widespread and a pest, their value dropping, so the age old method of poaching became more of a commonplace; two men, a gun dog and ferret being widespread. Further as local or larger rabbit plagues developed more and more, so, in the 20thC, the Myxoma virus was deliberately introduced as a control, being first found in the UK, in Kent in 1953 and reaching this shore in 1958-9 aided in this quickly national distribution by the deliberate and rapid spreading of the infection by interested farmers. So it seems, in tune with the fate of the once respected rabbit, so has the name of our local Headland waxed and then waned though, one suspects, there are many who would prefer its older and more appropriate working title and not the ugly and fanciful, Hengistbury.

IRONSTONE, IRONWORKS AND HARBOUR PLANS

2

Masses of ironstone exist in Hampshire, lying in the tertiary formations and in nodules in the London clay and Bagshot beds. Some is very rich (i.e. up to 50% iron) and has been used for centuries though sometimes as just building material as for example, in Roman Silchester's walls, though a Roman forge is known to have existed on Hengistbury.

The most important Hampshire ironworks of recent centuries were those at Sowley near Lymington. Here two considerable iron mills were in existence c.1787 and the ironstone which was smelted "was collected along the shores of the Solent" and also from the foreshore around Christchurch Head.

The site had soon drawn attention, in particular from Andrew Yarranton, in his book England's Improvements by Land and Sea (1687).

He said, "I found in the sea, great quantities of ironstones lye in a ridge. The stones near the shore lay so great and thick that they were the occasion of the lodging up of the sands near them." He also reported "that the King may have all his Iron made, and Guns cast at very cheap rates." There is Ironstone in the Sea by the Harbour mouth, and the King "hath such vast quantities of woods decayed in the New Forest, of which at this time charcoal is made and shipped to Cornwall and other parts. If two furnaces be built about Ringwood to cast Guns, and two forges to make Iron, and the ironstone be brought from the Harbour mouth out of the Sea up the river (Avon) to the Furnaces, and the charcole out of (the) New Forest to the works, there being sufficient of decayed wood to supply four ironworks for ever; by these means the King makes the best of everything ... and having ironstone of his own for gathering up, and wood of his own for nothing, he will have very cheap guns and iron."

A proverb in the South-West of the county; but one which has almost died out, is that "there will be rain when Sowley hammer is heard." Sowley hammer had not been heard for nearly a century (in 1887), but examples of the iron smelted and manufactured there may still be seen in the palaces at Beaulieu, whose shores also yielded ironstone "doggers". See T>W> Shore, The Old Ironworks of Hampshire, <u>The Antiquary</u>, May 1887.

Until the 19thC, however, little environmental damage happened through their extraction, that is before 1848 when a massive ironstone removal project got underway under the control of a Christchurch coal merchant J.E. Holloway. The extremely destructive erosion of the Head then began and continued to c.1870 by which time the environmental cost was almost catastrophic, the determined exploitation having defaced the mass of Warren Hill and removed all its natural protection of 'doggers'. Eventually, and triggered by Bournemouth concern, the Board of Trade for bad further mining but rather too late to avoid today's damaging continuing legacy fully detailed in <u>Ironstone Canyon</u> 1986.

HARBOUR PLANS

Over the centuries there were a number of proposals, some even half attempted, to 'improve' Christchurch Harbour and most concerned primarily with the position or repositioning of the Run outlet. In antiquity, Druitt considered that the river ran out, straight under the headland, the marshes we see today having formed more recently. However, the first real attempt to improve the outflow may be dated to the Clarendon Pier - a long jetty of ironstone 'doggers' - much still visible in the centre of the spit. This work involved a cut being made through "the Hummocks" and Smeaton suggested later, (in 1762) that this pier was probably to have been supplemented by a second, on the south west side. Later (in 1836), Armstrong thought the original river outlet ran out on the south side of the 'Long Rocks' and that they were put there mainly as a kind of scour preventer, i.e. to stop the dunes on the north side being washed away and hence the flow retreating northward - its most natural and usual course.

These works (of c.1695) were, nevertheless, the last on this coast for many years though it seems that before 1815, and for a fair period afterwards, the mouth of the river was stabilized at somewhere near the Long Rocks even though this cut was to be blocked by drift material by c.1730. Early maps from c.1720 tend to confirm this and it seems, even despite the pier's only limited efficiency, the mouth did not move much, North or South,, until c.1750. After this date, however, much changed and this, contingent on the beginning of the removal of ironstone 'doggers' from the foreshore which seems to have been an occasional activity before their wholesale removal began under the ironstone mining company from 1848. By 1836, therefore, Armstrong's sketch map shows the outlet to have removed well north, probably to its traditional route (as does Smeaton's 1762) which, of course, would best explain the siting of the Black House (of c.1600) when this was made guardian of the main harbour entrance. The period of greatest movement was then, probably 1750+ and it's from this time the sandspit began to build dramatically, as more and more drift material was created around the Head. By 1836, the spit was approaching closer to Highcliffe than in living memory and, from then on, for at least a century, things generally were going to get worse.

HARBOUR PLANS

ANDREW YARRANTON 1676, 1687   England's Improvement (includes Long Rocks or Clarendon pier - in 'hummocks' 300 yards long)

JOHN SMEATON 1762
(20.5.1762)

c.£5,000 to achieve some improvements including a pier or jetty or ironstone - near Long Rocks. 6' channel to be dredged to Quay.

JOHN SYLVESTER 1836
(September 1836)

Estimated cost of improvements £1,700. Dredging and fencing shoals. Public meetings in Christchurch, November 1836. 9.12.36 Provisional Committee formed. No action.

WILLIAM ARMSTRONG C.E. 1836
of Bristol (25.7.1836)

Survey of Christchurch Harbour. Confine River to narrow channel and new plans for piers. Estimated cost £6,000.

RINGWOOD, CHRISTCHURCH HARBOUR IMPROVEMENT 1845

the idea was to create a proper port for shipping - but, as usual, would involve much "dredging and banking". (The proposed deep water harbour was to be the Stanpit side). Estimated cost £55,000.

VETCH REPORT (Admiralty) 1854
26.8.1854. (The Board of Trade obtained the appropriate jurisdictions by 12.1867). The Board of Trade are said to have stopped the mining in 1870, through the Harbour's Dept.

Full enquiry and inspection into the **effect** of J.E. Holloway's despoilation of the Head by ironstone mining since 1848 - latterly using a tramway. Vetch saw the removal of huge quantities of Ironstone as an 'evil'

EROSION PROTECTION 1869

Cuttings at Double Dykes? are suggested by some.

WIMBORNE & CHRISTCHURCH RAILWAY. DOCK PLANS AT HENGISTBURY 1884

First mooted (15.11.1884). It was to run along the western and southern shores of Christchurch Harbour. Two short branches were proposed, making a loop to connect the present Christchurch Station with the new line near Tuckton.

JANUARY 1937

Light Railway under construction at Hengistbury.

FEBRUARY 1937

Extensive harbour dredging in process with the 'Priestman Tiger'.

MARCH 1944

Plans are formulated for Christchurch Harbour after the War - in particular to develop the place as a yachting centre with perhaps also a Haven Quay - Cherbourg passenger service in 60 ton boats.

OCTOBER 1954

A large scale investigation is undertaken to see if Christchurch Harbour could be improved. Avon & Dorset River Board.

BOURNEMOUTH'S FORGOTTEN CANAL

Though usually ignored in regional and local canal histories, the cut established (c.1850) between Christchurch Harbour and the Salterns, then pre-existing below Warren, deserves consideration and a special note.

It was made by the Hengistbury Head Ironstone Mining Co. to serve a small dock close under the hill. From thence a network of temporary tramway links (some earthworks of which are still visible) ran to the various excavations.

For a number of years the ironstone was removed along the 'canal' by substantial barges - some of which were shown on the letterhead illustration of the coal merchant who ran the operation, J.E. Holloway, as also the steamer he used named, the Carrs. From there the stone was taken on by larger vessels, as ballast, to Homfray's Iron works at Tredegar (via growing Newport) so linking Hengistbury dramatically with dynamic South Wales, a key centre of the developing Industrial Revolution.

The canal cut was, it seems, always tidal, there being no need for, or sign of, locks. Presumably it was thought unnecessary, with a relaxed return trade like this one to even consider investing overmuch in other than the simplest venture. Moreover a sealock, though guaranteeing 3 or so feet of water for flotation could have been both expensive and troublesome given the robust cargoes. This absence, however, should not blind us, to the considerable earthmoving involved in the 'canal's' 250 yd construction. It remains even today, a wide waterway and must have allowed a useful manoeuvrability whilst the main Saltern it linked could well have provided a site for the mooring of many more barges than just the few of the illustration noted (above). The small dock below the hill was, presumably, mainly used as a wharf and would have probably had some form of timber staging plus sundry derricks for loading. As such, on any animated day in the 1850's, it would have presented a scene curiously reminiscent of the Roman Hard and harbour recently discovered but closer to the Nursery shore - the passing of 1600 years being as nothing in this ancient place.

So viewed as a canal and rather more than just a river improvement or navigational short cut, we have at Hengistbury a significant part of an integrated (pre Somerset & Dorset) routeway system to the Bristol Channel viz via mines, rail, canal, barge, ship and, finally, rail again - all modes contributing, from even this deepest South starting place, to the main developing industrial arteries of 19thC Britain. So, seen altogether and in this way, here was no small achievement for the new users of the ancient scattered resources of an otherwise forgotten if picturesque heath.

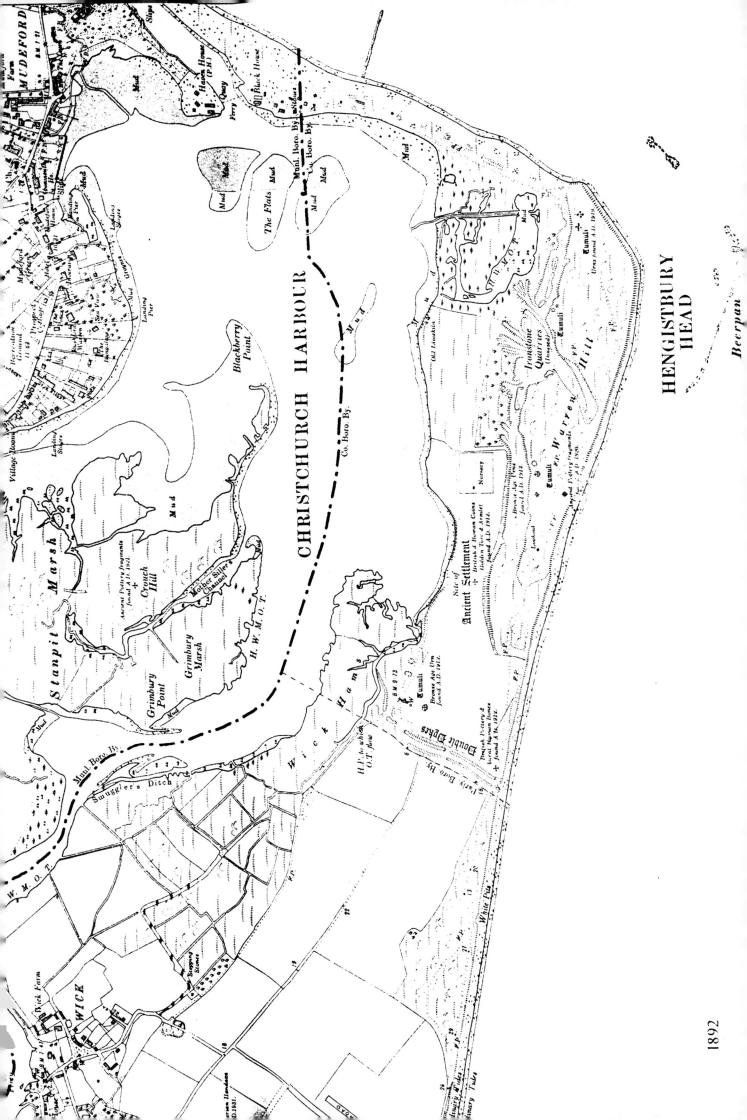

HENGISTBURY HEAD

CHRISTCHURCH HARBOUR

1892

3

CHRISTCHURCH FROM THE MID CENTURY

Christchurch in 1860

All must agree that the Christchurch of thirty years ago was not as the Christchurch of 1860 appears. The houses of that period had a weatherworn tinge, with dripping eaves and moss grown tiles, if not thatch coverings. The shops were few and of little account. Christchurch of 1860 has buildings erected, suited not only to the necessities of the occupants, but regard has been made to style, so as to render them ornaments to the town. Each shop that has been opened, rivals its predecessor in spaciousness and elegance and fitting. The Town Hall will long stand a memorial of the liberality of our kind representative and reflect credit as those who planned and aided in its erection. The Christchurch of 1860 is paved and lit with gas. The old houses are remodelled so that a roving son of Twyneham, sometimes sojourning in Australia, India or America, returning, may well exclaim "I should never have known it." Vast as the improvement is which has taken place in the space of a few years, there is much yet to be done.

Christchurch Times 15.12.1860

EVENTS IN CHRISTCHURCH (To 1918)

The <u>Christchurch Times</u> appeared first in mid 1855.

August 1856	Florence Nightingale holds a meeting at Christchurch Town Hall on Tuesday 19th August. A few days later the removal of this building from its site at the corner of Church and Bridge Streets for re-erection in its present position got underway.
June 1857	The original Ringwood, Christchurch & Bournemouth Railway plan is withdrawn because of the "unfavourable state of the money market." Lots of possible extensions considered had included a link along the coast to the Lymington branch (op. 1858) and to Salisbury - up the Avon Valley. All were 'contractors' lines', busy exploiting 'gaps' in the original network.
October 1858	W.S. Moorsom, is Engineer of the new Ringwood - Christhchurch line now in process. Thomas Brassey replacing Davidson in the first plan, is soon announced as the contractor. He was the leading railway builder in the country with Peto, second and Charles Waring third.
March 1859	Benjamin Ferrey is engaged on Priory repair work continuing to at least October.
April 1859	Whilst the Ringwood - Christchurch branch plan progresses steadily, the latter place is described as "a quiet and comparatively dull town." Tenders for removal and re-erection of Christchurch Town Hall are:- Messrs Eaton & Cottman, (Wimborne) £1,553 Mr. H.C. Tucker (Christchurch) £1,390 Messrs W. & H. Walden £1,370

	Messrs Belbin & Stone £1,353
	Mr. Wickham (Poole) £1,075 (Accepted)
	(Work all but completed by 18.2.60 and ready by 11.8.60).

August 1859   Royal Assent for RCB Bill.

December 1860   Christy's Minstrels appear at the Town Hall.

November 1862   The R.C.B. line opens, Thursday 13.11.1862.

October 1863   Mr. Bradford is the new landlord of the Railway Tavern, Bargates.

November 1866   The Rev. Zachary Nash directs the continuing Priory restoration.

July 1868   Tutton's Well. This had its origin in Cromwell's day. Old man George Touting - corrupted to Tutton. It is covered by every high tide and may still be seen beside the Stanpit Road.

August 1868   Death of Admiral Walcott - a local worthy.

February 1870   Mysterious disappearance of E.S. Elliott, a director of the RCB, which extension to Bournemouth opens on 14.3.1870 provoking a decade of hectic building there. It is a West Country town and so are its builders.

March 1870   The body of E.S. Elliott is found drowned in the Stour.

September 1871   The Regatta course is Claypool, Swinney, Branders Bank and the Quay.

March 1872   Proposed abolition of Christchurch fair.

January 1873   James Druitt (Coroner) holds an inquest at the 'Ship in Distress' Inn - the famous smugglers' pub at Stanpit.

Summer 1880   A pair of Ospreys regularly visit the Harbour despite the gunners.

August 1884   Several old tenements have been demolished for the purpose of forming a temporary road and crossing while the iron girder bridge over the railway is being constructed - a work which will commence in a few days.

September 1884   Drowning at Iford Bridge.

October 1884   The (new) railway Inn site is to be on the corner of Stour Road and Bargates. The hotel was planned "to be of an ornamental character" and was erected at a cost of £1,000 or £1,200.

November 1884   The possibility is 'dangled' before Christchurch of its being connected to the Somerset & Dorset Railway and Midland Railways by a line in a

N.W. direction towards Wimborne. (First Intelligence, 21.11.1884). A huge harbour improvement scheme is also outlined. Perry (of Southampton?) is the contractor for the new Christchurch Station. The route of the Wimborne - Christchurch Railway is announced. There is to be a wharf at Blackberry Point and a breakwater running 1,000 yards out to sea to the outer ledge of Christchurch Bay.

December 1884   Plans for the new Wimborne - Christchurch Railway were deposited in the Private Bill Office of the House of Lords on 17th December. The capital of the New Harbour Scheme is set at £1,400,000, in £10 shares.

March 1886   A fifth fatal accident occurs on the nearby railway works (20th). Joseph Firbank is now the main contractor locally.

July 1886   Legal action against Messrs Kellett & Bentley, previous contractors for the 'Direct' railway works.

Christchurch: The Castle Hill Ruins

'We understand on good authority, though it seems incredible, that the Town Council of Christchurch have resolved to pull down the remains of the unique Norman domestic buildings existing there near the Castle Keep, having obtained the permission of Lord Malmesbury and Sir George Meyrick to this 'improvement' in order to open up the view of the Minster. If this be true, and it's not too late to prevent the perpetration of such an act of vandalism, we hope the permission given will be at once withdrawn, at least until the opinion of competent archaeologists and antiquarians be obtained as to the historic value of the building. The Town Council of Christchurch have not long had the privilege of a charter of Incorporation and it is to be hoped they will not, almost on the threshhold of their existence, commit an act which possibly would be regretted, not only by those acquainted with the antiquities of the historic old borough, but by antiquarians throughout the country. A 'view of the minster' should not be opened up at the cost of destroying a building of undoubted antiquarian value. For the ruin, which is now nearly covered with ivy, is one of the few examples remaining in the country of Norman domestic architecture. Its beautifully rounded chimney is, Mr. J.R. Wise tells us in his work on the New Forest (which contains an illustration of the house), one of the earliest in England. To destroy such a building would be most regrettable, and it is to be hoped that the Christchurch authorities are not beyond the influence of a strong and earnest protest against the wanton destruction of so interesting a ruin.

<u>Hampshire Independent</u>, May 1888

June 1888   A possible demolition of the Norman House is mooted - one of the finest buildings of its type in the country. Meantime, the new Direct Railway will bring increasing numbers of tourists to the area.

November 1897   More and more 'outsiders' discover Christchurch and need to explore. See 'A Visitors Impressions' (below).

May 1903   A walk is to be constructed in Christchurch from the Castle to the Quay.

September 1906	The 'quaint custom' begun by Gustavus Brander's Will of 1785 - for a sermon to be preached on the third Sunday in August continues. It is to commemorate his survival from a serious road accident in Temple Lane, London in 1768.
November 1908	'Christchurch and its Charms' are widely advertised.
April 1910	Old Christchurch was a Bronze Age Harbour say experts.
November 1911	Christchurch absorbs Hengistbury head within its boundaries so gaining a seashore at last. During the present year (1911), Bournemouth Corporation unsuccessfully opposed the application of the Christchurch Town Council for an extension of the latter's borough boundary which scheme included the incorporation of Hengistbury Head within the Borough of Christchurch. This important change will shortly come into effect as the provisional order ... has passed both Houses of Parliament and now awaits the Royal Assent. See Bournemouth Graphic, 24.11.1911
January 1916	A constant passage of motors and motor vehicles is noted over Iford Bridge with no protection for foot passengers.
October 1916	A Rolls Royce belonging to Gordon Selfridge crashes in Barrack Road. His local H.Q. will soon be Highcliffe Castle.
November 1916	The highest tide within the memory of the oldest inhabitant of Christchurch was recorded following the severe storm on the 5th. "The quay was strewn with boats and pieces of boats. The water came up to and beyond the Riverside Tea Rooms, a boathouse belonging to Mr. Keynes was also wrecked." The year has seen many gales.
1918	The Christchurch Times ceases publication until 1925. Up until this year (1918) all the type had been set by hand.

HISTORY OF THE CHRISTCHURCH TIMES

This local newspaper forms a most useful adjunct to any study of the mid and late Victorian town and harbour area.

It was founded by three local men to provide an independent local paper viz. The Minister of the Congregational Church - the Independent Meeting House; the organist of the church and a local solicitor (?Aldridge).

The newspaper made its appearance in mid 1855 shortly after the abolition of the Government tax on newspapers and by 1858 was published, it proclaimed, by Henry Sharp - with Edward Lockyer.

Production began at 50 High Street but in the same year (1856) it removed next door to No. 49. George Marshall of West End, Christchurch, joined as Manager in 1864 and later, from 1869 to 1915 became proprietor and editor. He was a member of the local Council to 1910.

In 1880, the newspaper moved again - to 24 West End, Bargates and finally to its most attractive and long term local base at Bridge Street, hard by the Avon.

Eventually, the printing side of the business was acquired by Gilbert Reid & Charles Nutman c.1935, when the concern became a Limited Company and remained so owned to 1955 when it was in the hands of Harold Aldridge, E.P. Whittingham and F.E. Abbot. It continued as an Independent paper into the 1970's but eventually became merged with the larger local group.

Prior to this, there had been a pause in production from 1918-25 because of postwar difficulties. Before the war all the type had been set by hand but from 1925 it was lynotype. During the 19th C, much of the paper had been obtained from London in partly printed sheets upon which the local news was then added. By 1916 it was entirely produced in Christchurch.

CHRISTCHURCH TRADE & INDUSTRY   1850-1908

John Edward Holloway (A Christchurch Coal Merchant of Barrack Road) advertises Haswell & Lambtons, Wallsend, "The best house coals in the world are now brought to Christchurch by a steam tug and powerful barges. Aggregate weight 600 tons and constructed especially for the shallow harbour". 26/- per ton delivered (1.9.1855). The tug (The Carrs) continued calling until at least 1860.

These barges were used also to carry away the Hengistbury Head ironstone to Portsmouth - returning with household coal.

J.E. Holloway also freighted a vessel (the Perseverance) in Christchurch Harbour with a cargo of prepared building materials for John Lemmon of Australia (1853).

High Sherriff, Wadham Locke of Wiltshire, a local landowner, had G. Holloway make a boat for him at Christchurch. The men who built the vessel were later entertained at the Eight Bells Inn (November 1847) just previously another notorious Smugglers Inn. Shipbuilding is now established at Mudeford.

John C. Bemister, Marine Coal Merchant 1857-1908 is well established at the Quay, this built c.1870 in stone and redeveloped in 1907. His vessels included the 'Charlotte', 'Olive Branch' and 'Diamond Peter'. All unloaded coal at the Town Quay, and sailed regularly for Portsmouth with 36 ton loads (approx). This was stored in the large coal store at the Quay Head - a building not demolished until 1908. The Charlotte sailed, finally, in November 1906.

In May 1859, the sloop 'Lark' belonging to John & James Bemister was run into by H.M.F. Doris killing the brothers Hiscock - members of the crew. The Lords of the Treasury granted 10/- p.w. for the joint lives - to parents William and Mary Hiscock. By early June, the Lark had reached Christchurch and was under repair.

Christchurch brewery - Joseph King, July 1860.

Potter, Weare & Co. Mineral Merchants announced that G.A. Betteridge was now the sole agent for their superior coals - now selling at Christchurch Railway station at 22/6, 20/6 & 18/6 per ton for cash. G.A. Betteridge, High Street, Christchurch. (August 1863).

The North, Midland & Christchurch Coal Co. announce they have coals in stock at the Railway Station. Household coal at 24/- per ton. Chalk & Lime to order. G.A.. Betteridge, Agent. (October 1863).

James Bemister (Snr) retired in April 1868. He thanked his friends "for their favours over his 50 years as a coal merchant and general smith". He reported he had disposed of his business as general smith to James Hyde.

In October 1868, he applied for a licence to convert a house to be called the Bournemouth Hotel but despite residing in the town for over 20 years, was refused.

Coal Advertisement.   Arthur Briant, Office, Castle Street, offers coal at 22/6 per ton. (The late E.S. Elliott's office - a Ringwood-Christchurch Railway line director.)

Samuel Bemister   Elected Mayor of Christchurch 29th June 1878 (and again in 1885).

Fatal boat accident near Christchurch Quay involving the Charlotte - belonging to Bemister.

J.C. BEMISTER   Coal Merchant of Barrack Road, Christchurch. 'The only shipper of Wallsend in the town'. £1.2.0d per ton delivered, 'cut up fit for the grate.' 17.9.1881 and 15.10.1881.

In early March 1899, Alderman Bemister led the purchase of the wreck of the French barque - Marie Therese - by 'a syndicate of Christchurch businessmen' for £40.

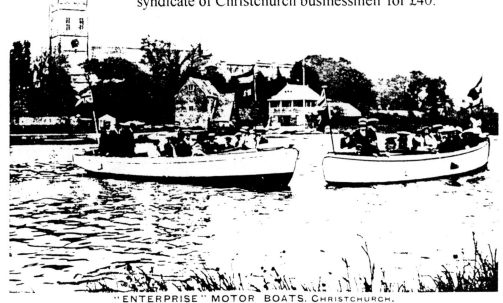
"ENTERPRISE" MOTOR BOATS. CHRISTCHURCH.

CENSUS STATISTICS - CHRISTCHURCH

Abstracts from 1871 and 1881.

<u>1871</u>

	Houses Inhabited	Vacant	Total	Population
Christchurch	1,868	84	1,952	9,475
Holdenhurst	854	42	896	6,043
Sopley	185	9	194	820
	2,907	135	3,042	16,338

<u>1881</u>

	Houses Inhabited	Vacant	Total	Population
Christchurch	2,681	308	2,989	12,989
Holdenhurst	2,014	253	2,267	15,648
Sopley	186	6	192	820
	4,881	567	5,448	29,457

Christchurch Population

1801	3,773
1811	4,147
1821	4,544
1831	5,344
1841	5,994
1851	6,251
1861	7,040
1871	9,475
1881	12,989

Note: <u>In 1881</u>, the population of the old Municipal Borough of Christchurch was 2,293, the town district of Christchurch 3,024, the Christchurch Rural Sanitary district 12,,,989 and the Parliamentary Borough 28,537. The Urban district of Bournemouth was 16,868 and the town of Bournemouth 14,940.

A VISITOR'S IMPRESSIONS OF CHRISTCHURCH.

A HINT TO OTHER VISITORS.

I have known Christchurch too many years, perhaps, to be able to point out its striking characteristics as they present themselves to the eye of the stranger, for (it may seem a paradox to say so) is it not a fact that a long familiarity with a place, or thing, possibly a daily acquaintance, lasting for many years, dulls the faculty of minute observation with regard to it?

However this may be, of one thing I am convinced, that visitors who dash over from Bournemouth, in noisy chars-a-banc, and drive " slap through the town," casting a careless glance on either side of the old High street as though it was of no account at all ; and hurry along to the Priory church as though it were the only thing we had to boast of! and, on the way back, while waiting outside the Ship hotel while the horses are being freshened up and the guard and driver get down to " stretch their legs,"—these visitors gaze around them languidly and with the air of poor bored-to-death folk.

Dear, dear, good people, do not hurry away yet! What have you learned of Christchurch by your hasty visit? The Church and the Castle, true, have had a few minutes of your attention ; but have you deemed the churchyard worthy of a quiet meditative stroll?

Have you leaned over the low stone wall of " Paradise," with its widening prospect, and watched the stream that flows slowly by at your feet and curves away to lose itself in the foliage of the adjoining grounds until it reaches the old mill at the quay?

Perchance you have had pointed out to you the grave of Water (sic) Spurrer, but have you expressed any curiosity as to the locality of Millhams bridge, where the ill-fated child, " his parents only joy," lost his life? Millhams Bridge is no more, and at the zenith of its existence consisted only, as we are told, of a plank or two spanning the shallow stream at the end of Millhams street, near the " Ship."

Am I wrong, too, when I suggest that St. Catherine's hill has not been honoured by a visit from you?

I expect you have heard, on the occasion of your visit to the Church, that it was here, tradition says, that the site of the foundation was originally laid, and the materials persistently removed to their present position, but have you journeyed thence?

St. Catherine's hill, be advised, is well worthy of a trudge over a dusky road for about a couple of miles, if you have a taste for a bird's eye view and a delightful show of heather, moss, lichen and bracken of every conceivable hue, and for wild undergrowth generally. Though the rugged grandeur of the spot, I warn you, is rudely disturbed and sadly marred by the presence, in recent years, of an ugly reservoir.

Rabbits abound ; and, like Robert in his walk on Camp Mount, my boys were here deceived by the counterfeit lameness of a lapwing, which rose at our feet.

The undergrowth is, indeed, most beautiful and luxuriant, and it is curious that it should find nourishment in such a sandy soil. The prospect on every hand is grand ; and amply repays the labour of ascent.

It is even said that the spire of Salisbury Cathedral can be descried on a clear day. That I cannot vouch for, though, certainly, we had a good view of the Isle of Wight and many miles of the surrounding country.

Mudeford,—as far away from the Church on the east, as our mount on the west—is well worth a visit ; not that there is much to see in the place itself, but the sea is here, and very good bathing can be had.

The point of interest to the artistic mind, however, is the little group of fishermen's cottages— huddled together, as if for mutual protection in stormy weather—on the small peninsula at the mouth of the Avon, and quite away from the road ; with a great stretch of backwater between it and the mainland, and bordered by pines. Here is Haven House inn ; and, if we are to believe the stories current, it is probably on this account that within good view of it stands a coastguard station.

But the erstwhile romance of deeds of daring attaching to Haven House has dwindled down to the less interesting and less profitable if more legitimate occupation of salmon netting and deep sea fishing.

Picturesque, indeed, is the spot ; and the old inn, its pitched walls and its ancient sign, almost obliterated by the weather of goodness knows how many decades, could doubtless a tale unfold!

Opposite, there is a sandy stretch with one or two other dwellings, also occupied by fishermen ; and, out at sea, boldly stands " the Island "—a faint grey with dazzling white cliffs.

To the right, over the river—which at ebb needs a skilful oar to stem the tide—rears Hengistbury (or Warren) Head : hence we will wend our way, requisitioning, however, a sturdy youth to take us over ; for the risk of being carried out to sea by the strong current of the " run ". is great, to the inexperienced.

The view from the Head, both seaward and inland is magnificent, and the breeze invigorating, blowing as it does straight from the Atlantic.

Keeping to the path at the edge of the cliff and making westward we soon get a good view of Southbourne and its pier ; then turning sharp to the right, through cornfields and lanes with high hedges and banks of blackberry, we pass a pond, emerald (in parts), with duckweed and dotted with snow-white waterfowl.

The ferry now soon comes in sight, with its tollhouse, tastefully built of rushes ; and a pert raven in a cage near by takes an intelligent interest in matters generally.

At the riverside a charming prospect lies before us, the Church in the background, with a mid-distance of green rushes, growing out of the bed of the river ; and the town quay, with its moored sailing boats on our right.

The ferry-boat is waiting, so we can cross over and enjoy the pleasing landscape from the other side.

Needless to say, salmon and other fish abound, but the rights are strictly reserved. Would they were not!

On our road from the ferry we meet a party of soldiers, and learn that there is an Artillery Barracks on the outskirts of the town, and that frequent gun practice takes place on the sands at Mudeford. On Sunday, we saw a detachment of the troops march to church.

Capital boating can be obtained, either at the ferry or at Tuckton bridge. The town also boasts of a small yacht club, and some excellent, if small, craft may be frequently seen sailing on the lower reaches of the river.

Blackwater ferry is distinctly picturesque, and should commend itself to the tourist ; as, indeed, should many another spot, all of which it would need a volume to indicate.

Suffice it to repeat that this historic old town has more to recommend it than its grand old Priory church, its castle, and its constable's tower ; that it has views and scenery at least as rustically beautiful as many another—perhaps " more fashionable "—resort, and that if visitors would only stay and honestly investigate for themselves they not fail to be as gratified and delighted with the result, as has been the writer after repeated visits extending over many years.

A. C. D.

4

AROUND WARREN HEAD

The earliest known names for the Headland are said to be Hednesburia (c.1107-1155); Heddin's Fort (14th C). Hynesbury (17th C) - by the time of the Dutch Wars 1666+. Warren came with the rabbits.

Hengistbury was a later construct but, as was noted by several writers over the years, a strong tradition had evolved around this promontory and the coming of Christianity to Britain.

In particular it was noted:

> 'Hengistbury' is the "keystone to Glastonbury. That Joseph of Arithmathea came to Britain via this place is a legend persistent in Somerset and Cornwall. Joseph was a merchant mariner trading with Cornish tin mines."

See, for example, <u>Bournemouth Times</u>
12.8.1938

Note: It is said that, as the Stour meanders far less than the Avon it was, accordingly, the preferred inland route of the earliest peoples - hence the round and long barrows common in Wiltshire.

AROUND WARREN HEAD
A Hengistbury Head Diary

May 1858	"I hear whispered about that the Government is intending to purchase Hengistbury Head and to erect two batteries thereon with stations for officers and men. That the men of the coastguard service have orders to be ready for work at a moment's notice." Telescope. (There is said to have been a lookout, plus battery here, before, during the Napoleonic Wars).
July 1858	A Sunday School ramble is held at Warren with "all kinds of sports and merry making."
September 1858	New Preventive Station. The Admiralty commissioners were reported to have taken a lease of about an acre of land at Stourcliff on the cliff near the late residence of Wadham Locke being part of Cellar Field Farm on which "they intend immediately to erect a Preventive Station". The term for which they hold the premises at the Avon Mouth will expire in a short time.
November 1858	Thomas Sherrick, one of the local preventive men, is accidentally killed (by a duck gun) whilst helping men climbing into a punt at Mudeford's Haven Quay.
January 1860	A substantial and clearly important road is marked on a contemporary map - running from Tuckton across the empty heath to Double Dykes

and Warren. It is joined by the track from Wick. This road was Broadway Lane and it must have had its origins in antiquity although its survival was probably far more due to smugglers, riding officers and fishermen. Interestingly in this period, there was no public right of way to the Head through Wick.

June 1860   Departure of the Great Eastern. Off the Needles 10.30 a.m. Sunday, June 17th.

The Great Eastern slipped her moorings in the Southampton Waters at 8 a.m. and although the weather was both thick and stormy she proceeded to thread the narrow and tortuous channel down the Solent and through the Needles, under the pilotage of Mr. Bowyer. The weather was far too thick and stormy to render it safe for her to have got away last night; perhaps it is as well she did not, as on passing Hurst Castle, a large troop ship could be plainly distinguished fast among the rocks near the Needles, no doubt having been forced there by one of last night's squalls. The wind, for our present course, is fair and everything seems to promise a good passage though perhaps not a very quick one."

Note: The Great Eastern (launched 31.1.1858) had been down Channel the previous year, at Portland in September 1859. (Brunel died on the 15th.)

May 1862   The Late Gun Accident at Wick.

Many will remember with regret the fatal gun accident which occurred at Wick in August last to Charles Edmund, age 16, youngest son of H.J. Smith, of Somerford, Magna, Wilts, who it was supposed, accidently shot himself by taking up a loaded gun while sitting on the cliff. A 'broken column monument' was erected recently (at Double Dykes) by permission of G. Gervis Bart. - contiguous to the spot where the accident occurred. The pillar was enclosed by iron paillisading and an inscription. (Note: Henry Smith was the owner of Stourcliffe House, Southbourne.)

May 1867   T.A. Compton later of Southbourne fame, writes about the weather in the locale.

September 1867   Marriage of Dr. T.A. Compton.

July 1868   The view from Hengistbury. You reach the top by the easy road 'cut up the side of the hill' and once there "stand by the side of the old Watch House which is the best point of observation." Landmarks include 'the celebrated 7 firs - for many years the landmark of our fishermen when dropping their gear on the Christchurch Ledge. Below - is Mount Misery, the chosen site for landing many of those rich (smuggling) cargoes.

May 1871	A small steam yacht runs on Christchurch ledge but is freed by the Tuckton coastguards.
July 1871	Southbourne Winter and Summer Gardens are located at Mount Misery.
October 1871	Southbourne Winter Gardens Company are 'Making out their projected roads.' 'A bridge over the Stour would be a great advantage' say supporters.
October 1874	The body of a young man was found on the Western Shore on Wednesday night (14th) by one of the coastguardmen at Tuckton which was then removed to the preventive station. Information was sent to Lymington where a boat accident happened on Saturday week (10th) and on Thursday afternoon the body was identified as that of Upson who was drowned on that occasion.
January 1877	"Ship Ashore. On Wednesday afternoon (3rd), a large barque had the misfortune to get on the shingles near the Needles during the heavy gale which prevailed all day. Minute guns were fired for assistance which was rendered as early as possible but grave fears are entertained as to the possibility of extricating the vessel from her most dangerous position. At the time of writing, it was feared the barque must go to pieces under the heavy seas breaking over her."
May 1879	A Lymington vessel goes aground on the Shingles - an area of very shallow water covering a moving ridge of stone near the Needles, the bar occasionally visible in freak conditions.
June 1881	Laying the foundation stone of St. Katharine's Church, Southbourne.
May 1882	The stern of the Alexandrovna is found near 'The Guns'. Also, the upsetting of a boat off Southbourne produces an inquest.
January 1884	The Hengistbury Head estate has housing plans passed.
March 1884	2 bathing machines and 3 bathing boxes (value £39) are destroyed by storms at Southbourne, the property of the new Southbourne on Sea Freehold Land Co.
May 1884	A Boxer rocket post is established at Southbourne.
August 1885	It is rumoured the LSWR is considering building a branchline into Southbourne - a possible response to the Wimborne & Christchurch Railway plan. Already a new railway harbour has been mooted for the Head (22.11.1884).
September 1887	"The quarterly practice of the coastguardmen stationed at Bournemouth & Tuckton took place, on Monday afternoon last (19th) at

Southbourne. 12 men, under Divisional Officer Herbert (of Swanage) took part in the practice which was in connection with life-saving apparatus. The movements of the men were watched with interest by a number of spectators."

May 1892	Hoare makes improvements to St. Katharine's Church in newly developing Southbourne.
September 1892	Sir George Meyrick's 'No Road' notices at Hengistbury Head are challenged. This was an attempt to bar the right of way which the Rev. L.R. Whigham (Vicar of Southbourne) said had existed for 50-60 years along the seaside. Apparently rabbits and their shooting was the only sporting right affected. It was said:- "To cut off (ladies and gentlemen) from the accustomed and harmless walks upon the Head is not true wisdom even if it prove good law."
March 1894	The worst storm of the century visits the Headland and Western Shore.
October 1896	An inspection of Southbourne coastguard station by Capt. Piggott of Alexandra. He was reported, 'well pleased.'
Oct./Dec. 1896	Recent heavy gales continue: casualties include 'Old Harry's Wife' near Studland.
December 1898	The 500 ton Marie Therese (a 3 masted brigantine) is wrecked inside the Beerpan Rocks at Hengistbury and soon becomes a total loss. She has the same owner as the Bonne Mere which was driven ashore, but recovered only half a mile away and the month before (viz. 24th Nov.). In a calamitous month, a raft from the wrecked Ernst of Barth was also driven below Warren.
March 1899	The sale of the cargoe of brickettes on the Marie Therese is sold to a syndicate of Christchurch businessmen for just £40. Meantime, the St. Katharine's Church works near completion at Southbourne.
June 1899	A unit of Royal Engineers camped on Warren Head attempt to blow up the wreck of the Marie Therese as part of a training exercise (26th). Lady Meyrick pressed the button.

Bournemouth Observer 28.6.1899

CAMP OF INSTRUCTION AT WARREN HEAD
blowing up a wreck.

On Monday morning (26th) large crowds of spectators assembled at Warren Head, it having been rumoured that an attempt would be made to blow up the wreck of the vessel Marie Therese which was stranded there some months ago. The rumour proved correct and it transpired that, for some days past the cavalry representatives, under the direction of the Royal Engineers stationed at the camp for purposes of instruction had been engaged laying mines connected by electric circuits with the shore, with the view to the destruction of the wreck. One hundred pounds of gun cotton were employed and shortly after half past nine the sound of the third bugle indicated to those assembled on the surrounding cliffs that something might be expected. Sir George and Lady Meyrick had previously arrived at the camp and on intimation being given to her ladyship that the time had arrived she pressed the button communicating the electric discharge and immediately was witnessed a tremendous discharge of shattered timber from the wreck. The demolition of the vessel was not so complete as had been anticipated but the explosion left it in such a condition that what was left undone by the work of the Engineers will be speedily accomplished by the first surf which the weather may create. Possibly another attempt will be made before the camp of instruction completes its period (at least since 3rd June) of residence here. No second attempt took place and the Marie Therese gradually fell apart thereafter. Many of its timbers were used to line the interior of the very distinctive house at 180 Windham Road, Springbourne.

c.1900+	During this period, the Head (like Swanage and district) was used extensively for army Summer training camps. The R.E. built numerous bridges across the 'Canyon' and surrounds and also on the marshes at Wick Hams. Bare-back riding and river sports were all part of these Summer expeditions.
May 1900	Locally, some correspondents were critical of the place; as when one wrote "As an occasional visitor to your ancient and beautiful town, I must protest strongly against the modern innovation of a practically open sewer which befouls one of the most frequented of the many lovely walks in Christchurch, i.e. to Warren Head. As they take no steps to alter or abate the nuisance, the least thing the Pokesdown Authorities should do is supply all intending visitors to Christchurch with clothes pegs and scent bottles."

Yours, E.E. Clarke, Parkstone.
14.5.1900

March 1901	Death of J.E. Holloway (aged 80) on 30.3.1901 who had established the disastrous ironstone mining works on Hengistbury in 1848, the central problem of the whole area. (See Ironstone Canyon 1986.)
February 1903	A body is washed ashore at Southbourne on Sea, opposite the coastguards station.
July 1903	The Summer camp of the Royal Engineers is held on the Headland. Soon one of the soldiers is to be involved in a sad drowning incident.
March 1905	More coverage of 'Warren Head' as a developing tourist place appears in local papers. Bremer is the 'Keeper'.
February 1906	Assistant Bournemouth Surveyor F.P. Dolamore notes how the 19th C. ironstone mining was "stopped by the Board of Trade."
March 1908	"The tragedy at Warren." Emma Sherriff (36) is found murdered on a lonely part of the cliffs between Southbourne and Warren Head

(21st/22nd). She had been strangled. An ex lifeguard, Frank Maguire, is the chief suspect but is later acquitted.

1911-1912	Archaeological excavations are carried out at the Head by J.P. Bushe-Fox. Sections of Double Dykes are made and this promontory fortress is stated to date to the same period as Dudsbury and Badbury Rings. There are 10 barrows, including a Long Barrow as the Head.
November 1913	Sir George Meyrick still permits the public to walk around the Head and sandbanks as before, on condition "they keep to the path provided and do not wander at all." There is, however, the grim prospect of bungalow development.
June 1914	Christchurch Head sees further achaeological excavations taking place.
April 1915	Just 5 years after the International Air Pageant below Warren, the area inside the Double Dykes is used for a military parade. Viz.,

"On Wednesday 21st April 1915 there was a ceremonial review of the 74th Infantry Brigade held between Double Dykes and Warren Hill. Several thousand people, including the Mayor, saw Major General Ventris inspect the troops. Those taking part were the 8th Loyal North Lancs, the 9th Loyal N. Lancs., the 11th Lancs. Fusiliers and the 13th Battalion Cheshire Regiment - all of whom were billeted in Boscombe or Southbourne."

August 1918	The Archaeological finds of the 1911/12 season are displayed at Hinton Admiral House by Sir George and Lady Meyrick.
November 1918	Gordon Selfridge, guest of Honour of Bournemouth Rotary Club, speaks about Christchurch Head. He said he intended "to make it a place the people of Bournemouth could enjoy as well as himself."
1919-24	The second main set of excavations takes place under H. St. George Gray. By now Selfridge has bought the Head plus adjoining lands from Christchurch Council.
January 1925	Rabbit diggers are active laying traps on Warren. The Christchurch Times will recommence publication this year.
May 1928	Death of Sir George Meyrick.
July & August 1930	The first plots in the move towards Hengistbury are sold, i.e., in Willow Way and Sunnylands. For 20 years since the Air pageant - these fields have been untouched, save as rough grazing.
September 1930	A.J. Seal produces an architect's plan for a grand marine drive all round the Head plus a bridge at Mudeford.

March 1931	There is an assurance locally that there will be no aerodrome created below Hengistbury Head. It is remembered that Selfridge imposed covenants against building - on all the lands before Hengistbury which he sold to Bournemouth.
May 1932	Nevertheless, by "common consent" Bournemouth Council's policy for the Head was deemed one of "non-interference". It was recognized that "the attractiveness of the Head consisted largely in its pristine beauty. Any park like layout would be not only unnecessary but detrimental." The only concessions were to be a few benches "dotted about".
August 1933	Despite the 'new' controls there are however "aerial thrills" this year, in front of Hengistbury.
September 1933	Hengistbury sees more coastguards activity: lifesaving practice etc.
October 1933	A body is found on the rocks below Warren.
November 1934	Two plans for local airfields are aired.
June 1935	Another military camp at Hengistbury including cavalry. J.B. Calkin, local archaeologist, says "The rise of London as a new economic centre in England and the establishment of a peasant population over the greater part of Salisbury Plain and Cranborne Chase struck a fatal blow to the prosperity of Hengistbury."
July 1935	Octogenarian Mrs. E.A. Jones (born 1851) remembers the blasting operations of the Hengistbury Ironstone miners. Her father, Captain Henry Dowling, was then stationed at the Old Watch House atop Warren (in the middle of the Head) - the whole place then overrun with rabbits. She says that, as a small girl, she saw "men go up the cliffs and set gunpowder. There was a great bang as the stones blew up. We found it safer to keep away from the cliff in those days."

She also noted how, even at the mid century, "a lot of smuggling was going on and the coastguard had to keep a sharp lookout." She, her mother and brother, kept her father supplied with coffee in this task at the Old Watch House - "one great room with 4 windows" - where they spent many happy days, even keeping a pet jackdaw "who stole anything."

The mining operations and the smugglers - often in disguise - provided continual points of interest plus wreck and rescue on the shore and, pretty soon, as the erosion increased, it became impossible to walk on the shore, right round the Head. On a return visit of nostalgia to the Watch House site c.1933, however, all Mrs. Jones could find on it were "a few stones" - and no longer, the numerous cattle and sheep there once were. The Watch House is said to date to c.1800 and was "occupied by a naval officer who looked after the adjoining signal station."

July 1936	Another walk around the Headland via Wick is chronicled locally. Now "great assemblies" appear on the Head helped to get there by the new Broadway.
January 1937	A light railway is under construction to facilitate the long groyne sea defence works £19,000.
February 1937	There is extensive dredging of Christchurch Harbour.
March 1937	The Roman Ford of Ytinga, near Double Dykes, is destroyed by the dredger.
April 1937	Locals begin to fear that Christchurch has "eyes" on Hengistbury Head and Wick including a ferry and some further development of Stanpit.
March 1938	It is said that plans for housebuilding at Hengistbury now do not envisage going beyond the line of Double Dykes.
April 1938	Despite the re-assurances, a petition circulates to protect Hengistbury Head from building. Altogether Bournemouth's push to the east is considered to be going "too close" to the Head. Moreover, the new Broadway is bringing a rush of visitors to the once lonely headland.
June 1938	A new bus service opens to Hengistbury.
January 1939	The new long groyne at Hengistbury is pronounced "a success".
February 1939	The Saxon King Hotel's licence is approved. There are now some 284 houses in this area plus this huge roadhouse on the Broadway.
March 1939	Southbourne's continuing erosion is deemed "a crisis". (see relevant section.) Meanwhile, the construction of any cafe as planned, near the end of the Broadway and Double Dykes is considered "the thin end of the wedge." Soon too, fears grow that the Ranger's Cottage here, "once a smugglers' haunt" may itself be demolished and replaced by a cafe. Numerous objections develop, led by the Southbourne Ratepayers' Association. "It can never be replaced", all agree.
May 1939	Motor coaches can now reach the Head. Tuckton and Wick are thought also to be 'threatened'.
July 1939	8,000 visitors descend upon the Headland on Whit Monday. A.L. Paris warns against further development - which might swamp and destroy it.

September 1939- May 1945	War intervenes to produce, rapidly, a massive change of use for the Head involving military training, rifle and assault ranges, considerable pill box building and later, in connection with 'beam bending'. A large naval gun is placed on (N) Double Dykes to guard the harbour entrance. Military tumuli and tall aerial masts cover the landscape as tourist needs dwindle to nought. In particular the land below Hengistbury and astride Double Dykes became the site for one of 50 coastal radar stations - part of the Chain Home system. Here scientists monitored enemy signals by means of 6 tall aerials/receiving towers - so both anticipating and helping to deflect attack. It was an extremely secret site, but the 'disfigurement' of the Head would take years to repair.
August 1945	The obelisk commemorating the accidental death of Charles Edmond Smith moved twice since 1862 and because of erosion, a total of 160', was now removed to St. James' Churchyard at the top of Pokesdown Hill.
May 1946	A debate develops over the "present condition of Christchurch Head" particularly as the public are revisiting an area still sown with mines and other explosives. The RAF sentries have now been withdrawn and, at a meeting in the guardroom, it is said to be "next to impossible" to keep people out even though the Head had not yet been de-requisitioned. A further search of the minefields was to be made soon.
August 1946	As materiel and other ordnance litters the Head, it is remembered how there was a battery atop the Hill in Nelson's Day, against invasion by Napoleon.
September 1946	Col. Paris makes a plea for the recognition of the Head's historic value. He moves that when the Military de-requisition it - the Parks Committee should mark the site. Paris avers the place was a key point of entry for Salisbury Plain and Cranborne Chase 2,500 years before he argues that, very probably, the Blue Stones for Stonehenge ended their sea journey here.
May 1947	Homeless families find a haven at Double Dykes in the several Nissen huts remaining there. For the 9 families this is to be "a homeless haven". Later, one of the huts, thatched! - is to serve for many years as a tea cabin (c.1952-73). Death of Gordon Selfridge. It is remembered how he sold the Head "to be preserved as public open space" for £25,250 (1930).
July 1947	The Headland is now declared "safe" and people could roam at will on it once again. A "methodical sweep" had been made by gunners of the 269th Heavy AA battery of the Royal Artillery "under the direction of

Lieut. J. Phillips, 19 men covering the Head in a line - during the last 10 days." Their finds had included sundry mortar bombs and hand grenades, no doubt a legacy of the time when the site was used as a "battle innoculation ground" for French Canadian forces. Throughout the war, the Head was used for mortar practice and as a field firing range.

Despite the clearance, however, the military did leave a lot of trace on the Head, especially lots of barbed wire and anti-invasion 'teeth' and other material which would take another decade, at least, to clear.

Even today, relics abound, spent bullets especially around the rifle range sites below Warren's western face. One young lad, once brought a box of hand grenades home, c 1956.

October 1947   Full details of the Old Tithe Barn at Hengistbury emerge, in particular that it may be the oldest inhabited building in Bournemouth. Now used as the Ranger's cottage it is occupied by Robert Brewer who had worked for Selfridge since the first war safeguarding the headland. All around lay considerable "war debris", but although in 1939 it had been proposed to demolish the structure - now it was rethatched. Interestingly, in the rafters was found the signature W.J.B. 1537 indicating a dating to at least Henry VIII's time with parts maybe older. Henry Fooks, estate thatcher for Sir George Meyrick carried out the rethatching work.

July 1948   Paris returns to his theme stating that Vespasian may have landed here while, in W.W.2, 'PLUTO' ran from the beach at the Head. (sic?)

May 1950   The Mayor of Bournemouth unveils a plaque to the first local residents - the Bronze Age villagers of Hengistbury's Barn Field. It is repeated how there are no historical associations with the Saxon chieftains Hengist and Horsa, "who never came this way".

September 1950   An ancient British coin is found on Hengistbury. ?Part of Britain's first coinage.

June 1952   As interest mounts in the local archaeology - a Bronze Age armlet is discovered.

December 1952   The vitality of the celtic settlement is given a new emphasis - i.e. its pottery, coinage, iron workings and harbour trade.

June 1958   A G.P.O. trench reveals evidence of early Bronze Age occupation. Much pottery and Samian Ware.

July 1958   Signs of changing times. The large concrete blockhouse and camouflaging hill (at Double Dykes) is removed as are the several nissen huts and other World War 2 relics. Meanwhile, G.P.O. workers prepare the beach at the Head to link up the Channel Islands' telephone cables &c.

December 1959   A Riverside walk is in process of formation.

October 1960   A heavy gale further damages Southbourne beach whilst floods swamp the Warden's Cottage by Double Dykes. 7,000 gallons have to be pumped out - all the product of torrential rain.

February 1961   Savoir Faire Magazine (F.W. Robins) focuses attention on the Archaeology of the Headland. Saxon pirates may have ended the port in the 4thC.

June 1963   Pontins opens at Wick Ferry (29/30th) after two earlier refusals.

September 1963   A proposal for a petrol station by the Saxon King is vetoed.

November 1963   More plans for the 'empty' lands include a Youth Training Centre at Wick Hams tip near Double Dykes and for the proposed Bournemouth University, to be sited on the approaches, nearby.

April 1965   There is the possibility of the demolition of the Haven Inn at Mudeford. Protests grow.

May 1965   Plans to dump household rubbish in the ironstone 'canyon' are vetoed.

June 1965   St. Katharine's School opens, near the top of Wick Lane.

November 1965   Stanpit Marsh's management plan is announced.

April 1967   Mudeford prepares to repel oil from the Torrey Canyon.

November 1967   There are further pleas to keep the harbour natural. Approx. 10,000 cars a year use the narrow lane to the spit. Permits were first issued in 1962 but the system was "much abused".

December 1967   Accordingly, the 'Noddy' trains (P.O. diesels) are introduced on the road at Hengistbury as an environmental measure. They meet some opposition and ambush!

March 1968   4 Noddy trains are now given the 'green lights' by Bournemouth Council while disquiet grows over the huts at the spit.

May 1969   A new marina scheme suddenly comes to attention - to be sited near the Marine Training Centre. It causes much local alarm but is eventually dropped.

April 1971   More archaeological finds by Christchurch Harbour shore at Barn Field are announced.

June 1973	Hengistbury now begins to attract colossal numbers of visitors. In anticipation of the increase, a new sunken car park is created together with an extensive new shelter, restaurant and ticket office &c. The Nissen Hut days are over - this cafe run for 21 years by Bert Brewer, whose father and grandfather were both gamekeepers on the headland. The proposed yacht marina scheme at Wick Hams, (above) first suggested 8 years before, is stopped by the D.O.E.
November 1974	Hengistbury Head is said to be eroding at the rate of 3' p.a. at the cliff top - the effect of many trampling feet. There is a move to set up a coastline commission.
Winter 1974	Hurricane force winds batter the Head and damage the old coastguard lookout.
January 1975	The white painted coastguard's hut on Warren Hill is to be replaced by a new and better sited lookout (i.e. to guard the Beerpans).
c. 1975	Big sand 'transfusions' are tried across Bournemouth Bay to make up years of losses.
April 1975	It is said the 'worsening climate' in prehistory drove the Reindeer Hunters off and that 15,000 years ago, the Head was an island, the Stour emptying to the west of it.
July 1975	Excavations for the new coastguard cabin reveal middle Stone Age flints.
November 1975	"Will the Ranger's Cottage be sold on the open market or used as a Rural or local Museum?" ask local people. It's suitability for a protection order is stressed.
January 1977	Over one and a half million people p.a. now visit the Head - more than the entire previous total for the 20,000 years of occupation &c. which the place has known. More protection is deemed imperative.
June 1977	The fear the Head may become an island means 2 new groynes will be made to protect Solent Meads. There has been serious damage here over several years with a 1.5 metre coast loss p.a.
November 1977	The then "uninhabitable, damp and bug ridden" Ranger's Cottage (Keith Turner - Ranger) and its future is debated. Fortunately, Bournemouth's oldest building is to be protected and restored, as potentially "one of Bournemouth's most attractive dwellings." More works of conservation are also given the go-ahead - including new pathways through Wick Hams and more protection for the Head's vital wood - Bournemouth's best.

March 1978	A new book by Barry Cunliffe records how the Head's community formed the first real town in the UK.
October 1978	There is a £100,000 plan to replace the causeway built in the 1930's to make the Long Groyne. More groynes and other works are proposed for the unprotected stretch from Solent Road to Double Dykes.
November 1978	Approx. 2 million people now visit the Head annually to its obvious detriment. A working party report urges a delicate balance of conservation of "one of the most important archaeological sites in the country" - a unique part of the Nation's heritage. There are plans to fence off the dune area at the Long Groyne and to make other barriers.
August 1979	Prof. Barry Cunliffe intends a further season of archaeological work next year. A 30' circular building has been found.
September 1979	Hengistbury is said to have been occupied from the 7thC B.C. to the 4thC A.D. and was at its most prolific and busy during the first century B.C. It was the U.K.'s first international trading port and hence critical for European archaeology.
November 1981	It is noted how the last three seasons have produced spectacular finds in the digs at Hengistbury. A network of organized roads has been found serving the many round houses of the busy port. It is the first townscape of British Archaeology" that has been revealed plus signs of a silted up Harbour - with trial borings made in the Iron Age. The next stage was expected to be an underwater survey of this harbour.
February 1983	The <u>Illustrated London News</u> focuses on the ancient tools made on Hengistbury 9-11,000 years ago. It is one of the "most informative prehistoric sites of Europe" they say.
October 1984	The local MP urges urgent coast protection works. Several feet have been lost to the coast each year and especially at Double Dykes. A Save Hengistbury Campaign begins.
November 1984	It is thought that Hengistbury could become an island in just ten years. Erosion is now very serious at Double Dykes. A £4.3 million scheme is mooted.
February 1985	Does a ghostly horseman haunt the Head? 3 people have seen it since 1982.
July 1985	It is announced that a Roman Harbour, complete with gravel ramps, platforms and dug out channel - with considerable evidence of the wine trade - has been discovered. Before the discovery this was to have been the last year of a 6 year archaeological programme but now it seems set fair to continue. The discovery is said to have "enormous importance".

Summer 1986	Although concerned with natural history, Brian Barnes' new book <u>Coast and Shore</u> features, on its cover, the ironstone doggers below the headland including remnants of the pre-war light railway.
August 1986	The British Museum devotes an exhibition display to Hengistbury Head and its pottery and artefacts. Oil rig explorations begin in the bay. Will the Head become an oil terminal?
September 1986	The first coast protection works since 1937/9 are expected to take until 1992. Whitehall pays 60%. There are pleas to make the Tuckton - Hengistbury riverside a green belt.
December 1986	There is another proposal to close down the beach huts at Mudeford and so to return the site to nature. Also to stop buses running to Double Dykes.
January 1987	A further report is published on the deteriorating condition of Hengistbury Head: A 77 page management plan which stresses sea protection works and also a reduction in visitor numbers by more focus on the Solent Meads car park and beach nearby.
October 1987	The latest stage of the coast protection works at the Head is deemed complete. The £3m has gone to provide 5 new groynes and a causeway near the Long Groyne - an area, recently, much the victim of the sea. The first priority was the 200 metre barricade made at Double Dykes plus beach shingle replenishment.
May 1988	There are fears that Hengistbury could be "spoilt beyond repair" by the huge numbers of visitors. Suggestions include reduction of the car park by two-thirds and an end to huts on the spit.
March 1991	The beach huts at Mudeford are exempted from Poll Tax. Long term plans envisage their complete removal. Meanwhile, the Double Dykes are rebuilt, new paths made and several areas fenced off.
October 1992	New and expensive sea protection works are planned to save Mudeford in the face of continued erosion and global warming.
December 1992	The possibility of closing the Broadway beyond Rolls Drive is mooted.

5

FORGOTTEN WICK AND ITS RIVERSIDE

This little village, situated on the banks of the Stour but not far west of its confluence with the Avon to form Christchurch Harbour, was and remains the first and last settlement on the South side. It is very old, probably Roman in origin but certainly Old English and, most of all, important as a routeway, first by ford and later by ferry, to Christchurch and beyond, early access being mainly along the beach road from Poole and the West.

Its story is already the subject of a detailed monograph but to this may be added now a brief record of its mainly 20thC. history and here mostly the chronicle of the mounting pressures on its riverside. Wick still continues to appear in local news despite its now enveloping suburban quiet - most recently concerning the ferry which, withdrawn for two years, is expected to recommence at a rebuilt landing stage in Spring 1993.

We may begin, however, by just noting something of its 19thC. population as contained in the 1841 census.

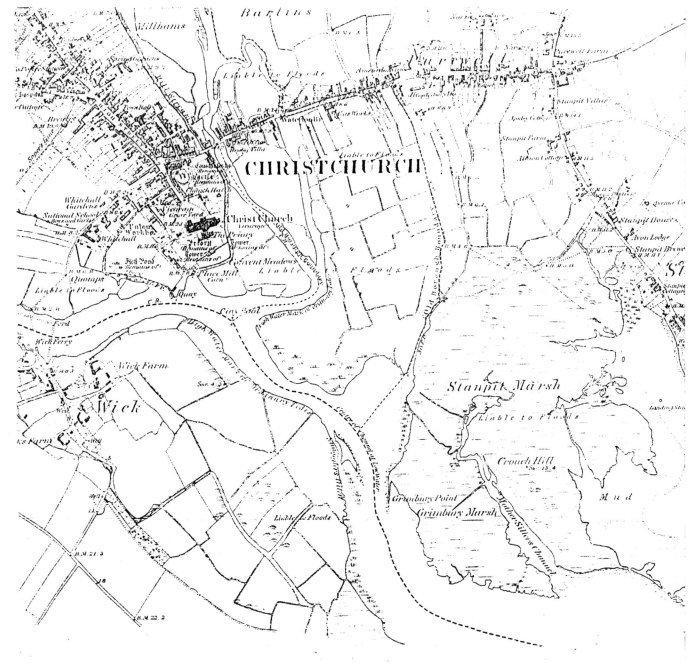

1841 Census Wick Tything of Tuckton

Name	Age	Occupation
John Sloman	30	Farmer
Louisa Sloman	25	
John Sloman	10	
Louisa Sloman	8	
Sarah Phillips	20	servant
Sarah Haslett	30	servant
Henrietta Dymott	25	servant
William Barnes	20	Labourer
Charles Quinton	15	do
Mary Veal	60	Independent
Elizabeth Brinson	12	
Ann Pain	80	Independent
Hannah Pain	35	do
James Pain	35	Ag. lab.
John Pain	45	Ag. lab.
Maria Pain	13	
Ann Pain	40	
Michael Brien	60	Army pensioner
Thomas Brien	20	Ag. lab.
Mary Brien	20	
Fanny Brien	15	
Ann Brien	3	
Elizabeth Brien	4 mos	
George Parsons	40	Ag. lab.
Sarah Parsons	45	
Jane Parsons	14	
Lear Parsons	12	
Eliza Parsons	8	
William Bendle	40	Ag. lab.
Harriett Bendle	60	
James Bendle	16	Ag. lab.
William Bendle	14	Ag. lab.
Elizabeth Bendle	10	
Mary Ball	75	Independent
Caroline Brinson	15	servant
Anna Brinson	10	
John Somers	30	Ag. lab.
Jane Somers	25	
Ann Somers	5	
George Somers	3	
Eliza Somers	8 mos	
Robert Bishop	35	Ag. lab.
Rebecca Bishop	35	
John Bishop	9	
Mary Bishop	7	
Ann Bishop	5	
George Bishop	3	
Elizabeth Bishop	1	
James Parsons	30	Ag. lab.
John Marshall	75	Ag. lab.
James Marshall	40	Ferryman
Eliza Marshall	20	
Stephen Marshall	45	Ag. lab.
Thomas Marshall	15	Ag. lab.
Levi Groves	20	Farmer
Marianne Groves	20	
Levi Groves	8 mos	
Ellen Frampton	15	servant
George Groves	20	Farmer
Charles Pain	25	Dairyman
Henrietta Pain	25	
Ambrose Pain	6	
Caroline Pain	4	
Anna Pain	3	
Sarah Pain	1	
Jesse Pain	3 weeks	
Sarah Vivian	20	servant
Marianne Wheeler	20	Nurse
George Barnes	40	Ag. lab.
Marianna Barnes	40	
William Clark	35	Ag. lab.
Elizabeth Clark	35	
George Clark	14	Ag. lab.
Sarah Clark	10	
Levi Clark	7	
Henry Clark	3	

Bournemouth Observer, Sat. 5th May 1888

The late Mr. Eli Miller of Wick Ferry.

The sudden death of Mr. Eli Miller after a few days' illness will, we feel sure, have been received with universal regret by all the inhabitants of Christchurch and its neighbourhood.

It is little more than a year since the older Mr. Miller passed away at the ripe age of 85, and now his son, when yet in the prime of life - he was within a few weeks of 50 - has been taken from the midst of his busy life, and from the faithful performance of those duties and occupations which were so dear to him.

To the many who are drawn to the Wick Ferry in the course of their daily toil, or in the pursuit of congenial pleasure on the water, the short sturdy figure sending his punt across in an unerring line, the face rugged but sagacious and intelligent, were thoroughly well known during the daylight hours; and after sundown the cheery 'jodel' and the flashing lantern from the other side were ever inspiriting to those who had walked across the damp meadows, compelled to cross the water after their long days' work.

All have recognized the industry, peculiarly his own which surrounded him with a fleet of boats; the sense and power of management with which he would arrange and despatch parties of pleasure in the fair Summer days; the facile dexterity with which his hands were ever ready to pare an oar, to alter a stretcher, to grease a rowlock; in fact to shrink from no work light or heavy which should ensure the success of whatever he had before him at the moment.

Early in his life Mr. Miller had turned his attention to the stars, and prompted by a desire to scan the mysteries of the heavens, in his leisure moments he constructed, with the assistance of a friend, a large reflector 'telescope' of considerable power and usefulness.

With the aid of this instrument, in hours stolen from sleep, Mr. Miller became something more than a mere amateur at the stars, and as a member of the Liverpool Astronomical Society was often in correspondence about the "spacious firmament on high" whose starry inhabitants he knew by heart. Moreover, the energy of mind which first bent itself upon the heavens was not restricted to astronomy alone. Eager for information on every subject of natural history, of science, or of art, Mr. Miller spared no opportunity of increasing his store of knowledge and did not hesitate to plunge into the writings of men such as Darwin in his search after truth. As an example of his fondness for observations of natural history we may mention that within a week of his death, writing to a person in the north of Scotland, he asked for all information about any Spring or migratory birds, because, he said, "I am much interested in finding out all I can about them."

To the artists of Wick Ferry, his keen enjoyment of natural beauty was often a source of wonder and admiration. On their return from work at the close of a day's toil the questions often put to them were: "Did you see the sky and the clouds about 4 o'clock, Sir?" or "Did you see the sunset this evening and its reflection in the east?" While, whenever he ventured to criticize or admire, his remarks were on many occasions useful and to the point. Only within the last few weeks he had begun to dip into and enjoy the fascinating writing of Mr.

Ruskin. With all this not inconsiderable store of knowledge gleaned on every side, there was never a trace of any intellectual affectation about him; he wished for knowledge, not to parade, but to possess it. For us who remain, the future, perchance, may bring changes in the scenery of the neighbourhood of an undesirable nature; who can tell? But while the beauties of the Stour remain untouched by progress, while the old willow with each returning year dons its livery of green, and casts its flickering shadows over the thatched hut on the landing stage; while the grand old reed bed annually discards its Winter dress of golden glory, and, assuming the rich greens and grey of Summer, tosses its fairy plumes to the sky; while the little backwater in each recurring June is starred with lilies, its banks with meadowsweet and loosestrife, is it too much to hope that those of us who visit and re-visit with ever-increasing pleasure these beauties, our common joy, will not forget, for many a year to come, sometimes to give a kindly thought to the memory of the kindly ferryman?

Salmon Fishing Near Christchurch   1889

Col. Brander's net caught 9 Salmon during the week ending on Tuesday (11th June 1889). 34 Salmon and one trout were caught in addition, the heaviest fish weighing 37lbs.

Bournemouth Observer 15.6.89, Sat.

Note: Col. & Mrs. Brander & family lived at Spiekers in Belle Vue Road, Southbourne (1889).

WICK

March 1890	Even at this late date the road between Tuckton and Wick was in poor condition with new works needed. Questions were asked who owned the land beside it as it was claimed by Sir George Meyrick.
	There were 2 more swans added to the riverside between Wick and Christchurch Quay which it was hoped would add to the picturesque quality of the local scenery. Only 1 of 4 survived from a group placed earlier.
December 1890	Wick Ford is declared abandoned as it had "not been used for many years" but traces will remain until the 1920's.
August 1891	A son of the local Dr (Hartford) got into difficulties when he slipped off the river bank near Wick Ferry. He was saved by a gentleman visitor.
September 1891	It is now said to be impossible to repair Wick Ford. Interestingly the Christchurch sewer outfall was just at the Ford site.
November 1896	No repairs to save Wick Ford were now envisaged.
October 1897	Sir George Meyrick agrees not to help resuscitate Wick Ford. As the largest landowner in the area and very concerned locally, he had the power to do so if necessary.

June 1901	Death of Major Sloman. Major Sloman died at Wick House on Monday night (3rd) after a few hours' illness. The deceased gentleman was in Christchurch on Monday afternoon, apparently in his usual state of health. Major Sloman who was a son of the late Mr. John Sloman of Wick was an army veteran, he having retired 30 years ago as a Major of the 61st Gloucester Regiment. He had seen service in many parts of the world. (born 31.7.1830, d. 3..6.1901.)

BOATING ON THE STOUR IN 1903

"If you want to know the best stretch of water in the district for a row" said an old boating man to me "go to the Tuckton Creeks." The Stour is well known as a boating river, and that portion round about Christchurch is specially delightful. The stream itself is of good depth, and broad enough to allow passing room, while the scenery is some of the most picturesque in Hampshire.

"The proprietor of the Creeks," he went on, "has provided what has long been needed, a supply of really good river craft. There are no disreputable tubs such as you find at nearly every riverside boathouse; everything is new and up-to-date."

I made my way to Tuckton Creeks one fine morning last week. Going by 'bus to Southbourne, a ten minutes' walk brought me to the toll bridge, at the Southbourne end of which is the boating station of which my friend had spoken. My attention was first attracted by a good-sized vessel, which stood high and dry on the bank of the river, hoisted on a concrete stand. This vessel, built by White, of Cowes, more than seventy years since, and for half-a-century employed in trading between the South of England and the Channel Islands, was placed in its present position about two and a half years ago by Colonel Brander. It is now used as a pavilion, the deck being furnished with seats and tables. Here a charming view of the fine old Priory of Christchurch on one hand, and the upper stretches of the river on the other is obtained; and the visitor, while choosing his craft, or taking his ease after a spin up stream, can enjoy the weed and luxuriate in light refreshments of various kinds.

Notwithstanding what I had been told, I was surprised at the quality of the boats on hire. They are all Thames skiffs of the very latest pattern, single and double, well fitted up and comfortably, not to say cosily, upholstered. There is also a good supply of Rob Roy and Canadian canoes of all dimensions representing the maximum of luxury and the minimum of labour. I saw one or two fine punts at the landing stage and was greatly surprised to learn the Stour thereabouts was quite puntable.

July 1901	Narrow escape from drowning. A boating accident just above Tuckton Bridge took place (on 13th) when 3 people in a 'Canadian canoe' got into difficulties but were rescued and rowed to the ferry.
August 1901	A well known local resident (Reeks) makes a final appeal for the repair of Wick Ford.
September 1902	Thomas McArdle of Wick Lane is summoned for allowing 4 cows to stray on Stour Road on August 25th.

June 1903	Mrs. Miller puts Wick Ferry (and its boating facilities) up for sale. It is said to have probably been here and in use "before the college of the Augustinian Canons was founded." The auction did not reach its £1500 reserve, however, and the lot was withdrawn. In 1838 the landing place was at the end of Sopers Lane but had migrated over time.
September 1903	Serious accident (24th) to Mr. W. Reeks of Wick Farm. Dr. Hartford attended.
July 1904	Serious boating accident opposite Quomps, near the Swinney Hole, Wick. Three boys (including a son of Christchurch photographer Mallet) were drowned while swimming from an island. The hole here was 12-14 ft deep and 30 yards wide. Many school boys bathed unsupervised.
March 1906	During the coming Summer, it was announced a service of motor boats would ply from Wick Ferry - calling at Christchurch Quay and to the harbour mouth - so saving the difficult 'row' back against the tide. Weeds in the river remain a problem however.
Summer 1908	More and more popular boating takes place on the Stour.
September 1916	Will of R.H. Carter Esq. RN of Wick. Paymaster. R.H. Carter RN of HMS Defence was killed at sea on May 21st. Aged 33. He was the eldest son of the late Rear Admiral Richard Carter of Wick and left property worth £1,586.
August 1921	Christchurch Regatta is held on the 10th. It had restarted again, after the war, in 1920.
Summer 1922	Wick Ferry Riverside Camp is run by proprietor, Jack Edmunds (Bill Bryant before).
January 1923	Upstream, Blackwater Ferry sees its last passengers.
January 1925	Wick Ferry is suspended for 5 days because of severe flooding and gales.
July 1925	For 5 years now the Christchurch Congregational Church have held their Summer fete in the grounds of 'the Meadow' by Wick Ferry, home of Mr. & Mrs. Walter Hoare. Their extensive river fronted site proved ideal for the purpose.
August 1925	Three youths from the area, Leonard & Alfred Kendall of Wick and Edward Napier of the Coastguard Terrace, Southbourne, challenge the Private Fishing Rights held on the riverside between Tuckton Bridge and Wick. They have ignored the notices saying Private (i.e. Exclusive) Fishery and determinedly pursued some eels.

Bournemouth Guardian 27.6.1903

The History of Wick Ferry

The history of Wick Ferry is quite a romance in its way. As there had been some suggestions made that the ferry rights were not the absolute property of Mrs. Miller, whose face must be familiar to thousands of local people who hire her boats in the Summer time, her solicitor, Mr. H.T. Trevanion, at the recent fruitless auction (Mon. June 22nd 1903), at the Kings Arms Hotel, Christchurch) of the property gave a brief narrative of the Vendor's title to it. It is quite a family history, going at any rate 90 years back to the ferryman named Marshall. On his death, the ferry was taken over by his son-in-law, James Miller, and at his death to his son Eli Miller, and since conducted by Mrs. Miller, the widow. We remember Eli Miller very well, and can certainly speak to the family being in receipt of the ferry fees as long ago as 1871. That runs very close to the statutory 35 years unmolested title, which we should imagine was clearly established. There is only one drawback to the use of the ferry by cyclists and that is the locked gate that bars the footpaths to Christchurch. Cycles cannot be taken through a V shaped wicket gate and it is troublesome to have to lift them over a five barred gate. Why the gate should be kept locked we are unable to say.

Christchurch.   Wick Ferry.

A Wick (ed) Incident.

Archie took three peachlets
To the Ferry for a row.
He asked them all to go,
For he wished to make a show.

But when the party reached the boat
Poor Archie looked quite blue.
He found he'd left his purse at home—
Now what was he to do?

WICK HOUSEBOATS & RIVERLANDS

February 1926   The mile long walk from Wick to the sea is popularized.

June 1926   Wick Lane to the ferry - "the loveliest spot around", bowered by elm and oak and with "holly bushes galore", beyond Broom Close, becomes the subject of concern, observers noted the "hand of the builder (was) already plainly at work. On the open space, on the Bournemouth side of Wick Lane, wooden pegs at regular intervals (told) their own story." The new estate was "to be dignified by the name of 'Brightlands'." Meanwhile, on the other side of the lane, work was "already in hand dumping soil right down to the river's edge." Hence, it was thought, "the riverland (was) to be such no longer, as river frontages, one learns from a (notice) board, are now available for houses." The development was considered "inevitable" but still "a thousand pities that yet another beauty spot, with magnificent trees, has to make way for riverside frontages."

October 1926   It is hoped to lay out Quomps as a recreation ground with gravel paths &c.

Summer 1927   Wick Ferry Advertisements appear widely - as for example, in the Christmas Official Guide.

January 1928   Severe floods, early in the month, affect the whole Stour Valley.

Summer 1930   The General Store is well established in the Village Centre by this period.

April 1933   Real concern develops over the fate of Wick Lane consequent upon all the new local building activity.

Summer 1933   Wick Ferry Riverside Camp, J.C. Edmunds (proprietor).

August 1934   Village Green celebrations. Smocks and local personalities parade.

July 1935   Sir Alan Cobham holds an air display at Wick.

January 1944   Christmas party at Wick. Through the kindness of Miss A. Locke 'all the children living at Wick were able to have a Christmas party.'

July 1944   A swimming pool is planned near Wick Ferry.

June 1947   Motorboats replace punts at Wick Ferry.

September 1953   There are objections to Council Flats being built at Wick.

June 1954	'Tin Can Driver' (George Cockles) determines to dive for Sam Hookey's 'treasure'. Permission is granted by Bill Warner - proprietor of the Wick Ferry Holiday Camp and a local resident.
June 1954	A family of 3 is saved at Wick when their rowing boat is holed.
August 1954	McArdles self service Holiday Camp is now well established.
September 1954	The scheme for the Riverside Walk in the Bournemouth Development plan develops. Negotiations begin, to open some remaining private sections.
December 1954	There are voluntary evacuees from McArdle's Holiday Camp Caravans at Wick following the floods of 27.11.54 (to Druitt Hall).
May 1956	A threat develops: homes at Wick. Bournemouth Council considers them insanitary and a 'blot' on the riverside. The occupants had had the privilege of living in them since the war plus "all sorts of sheds and huts". 30 or 40 families are given "one more year". Meanwhile, during 1956, Wick Ferry continued a deficit.
January 1957	A young couple who got their eviction order on Christmas Day to move their houseboat from the Riverlands Estate at Wick are given a 6 month reprieve.
February 1957	The Wick riverboats seem set to become a saga. An extensive agreement is made between their owners and the Corporation which will allow them to stay to November 1959. They are to have 3 years, effectively, to find somewhere else.
March 1957	The houseboat owners form the Wick Houseboat owners association. Two have been given a 6 month notice to quit.
July 1957	Two 'flying saucers' are sighted locally, one, a bright stationary high level luminous object over Hengistbury and another above a riverboat at Wick.
	Wick Ferry Co. is on a five year lease but needs 80,000 visitors to run again. It is operated by R.W. (Bob) Bishop, a well known local fisherman. A footbridge alternative is considered. A Riverside Walk on both sides of the Stour downstream from Tuckton is now under consideration. The 30th June last was the last day for the remaining houseboat dwellers to move their boats from the harbour. Many are large converted landing craft and MTB's.
	There is to be also a general 'tidying up' of the land on the Bournemouth side. At this time it was owned by William Charles Mills

but was in the process of being purchased by the Corporation. Mills had a small boatyard there for about 27 years but he had cleared all his stock by this date.

December 1957	As Bournemouth Council wanted to keep Wick Village centre "around the green, more open than built upon" they refuse planning permission for a bungalow on a site "previously approved for a piggery for 30 pigs". As they said, "the Council had been fighting not too successfully, a rearguard action against speculative builders in "the picture postcard village."
February 1958	Severe flooding of the Stour plus blinding snow and blizzards.
March 1958	George Taylor, occupant of Georgian Wick House, from c.1950, had an apology from the Council after carrying out some conversion work (to 4 maisonettes) of the listed (May 1952) property. He had only removed some worm eaten panelling.
June 1958	There is a proposal to make the Riverlands area of Wick into "a boating and sailing centre." The plan follows the expiration of 3 year old leases to MTB owners. Bournemouth Corporation had now bought all the Riverland from Tuckton Bridge to Wick Ferry. Meantime, the houseboats down to Wick Ferry could stay a further 3 years but one family, who had lived on the 'Queen Dolphin' for approx. 3 years, moored opposite the ferry, were selling and going to Australia.

By this month also it was hoped to fill in the inland creek near Tuckton Tea Gardens "to a point near Broom Close" and to do this by the end of the year. Also a woodland path was to be made to meander alongside Wick Lane, but with the hedges kept to preserve the rural (and locally still quite wild) atmosphere.

The rest of the creek was intended to be filled in by the end of 1961 with new sailing and boating facilities established at the Wick Ferry end. |
January 1959	More flooding at Iford and Wick.
June 1959	Local VIP's view Christchurch Harbour 'to deal with the problems raised by increased use."
October 1959	The houseboat dwellers at Wick continue to make news. After they have gone a 30 foot length limit for moorers will be established.
December 1959	The straightening schemes continue in the Riverlands. "The Stour now flows along a new cutting across the mouth of a horse shoe bend which is being filled in with hundreds of tons of household refuse." Meantime, the floods this Winter on the Stour are the worst for 8 years. The MTB's weather all storms.

August 1960	'Wick wives' say we stay put even though the houseboaters water supply is cut off by request of the Council on 10th August. It is said the people have had 3 years to leave, their MTB's taking up "too much space". The moorings are wanted for smaller craft. Letters of protest pour into the press - over Wick and its "waterless". People wash their children in River water.
September 1960	Police carry out life saving practice at Wick.
Winter 1962/3	There were 2 severe blizzards, on 31.12.1862 and 2.1.1963 after which everything - including the River Stour - froze solid for the better part of 3 months. This was the hardest winter since 1947.
March 1963	The new Wick Ferry Holiday Camp has several blocks almost completed. Planning permission was granted "at the third time of asking." Wickmeads, Bournemouth Corporation's 17th home, is opened next to Broom Close library.
June 1963	Fred Pontin offers his campers a free holiday at the new building opposite Wick Ferry because at this point it was only a concrete shell for the ballroom. 3 weeks to complete. Christchurch Corporation is to enter discussions on any future developments in the harbour.
July 1963	The 10 week "rush" to build Christchurch's restaurant cum ballroom (90' x 53') ended with its completion on 29th/30th June when it opened as the Wick Ferry Holiday Camp - "without ceremony". (Manager: John Lewis.) Drinks served on Monday 1st. (For details of how Pontins came to Wick, see inter alia F. Pontin, Thumbs Up, 1991, pp. 60, 78, 108.
November 1963	The Wick Hams rubbish dump is well established following the 'landscaping' near Tuckton Bridge. A Youth Training Centre near Double Dykes is planned.
Summer 1965	St. Katharines School opens at the top of Wick Lane.
October 1965	Now Pontins becomes a Holiday Village and no longer just a holiday camp; people now "merely rent a chalet and provide their own catering." Earlier in 1965 the adjoining caravan camp was acquired and 74 new chalets erected. A swimming pool was planned for 1966. Mr. W. (Bill) Warner saw the potential when he had lived on the other side of the River at Wick House. Wick Ferry was the first Pontin site to be converted to self catering holidays.
November 1967	The future of Christchurch harbour is under consideration again. There are to be new dinghy sailing facilities at Wick Hams and at Mudeford plus "just limited rounding off of existing building developments and carefully controlled wildfowling." A 'whittling down' of the beach huts

on Mudeford Spit is intended. It is said "the extension of urban development eastwards of Wick and Southbourne would destroy the character of the harbour. The Mudeford sandbank beach huts were harmful to the open character of the area and prominent against the skyline." A ban on cars to the spit is also proposed - resulting in the appearance soon, of the Land Train.

May 1969   A Marina Scheme for 200 craft is proposed for Wick Hams. A large opposition soon develops complaining of the "constant pressure" on this wild country and of the implicit "huge disturbance to wildlife."

August 1969   The views of the River Authority are sought by the Council over the Yacht plan.

September 1969   The new Noddy train (a G.P.O. tractor) on Hengistbury is 'ambushed' by raiders.

Bert Young - the Wick Ferryman - recounts his adventures from commencing at the riverside in 1913 (Aged 13) when passengers were poled across. These punts continued to c.1945/6. Young was in the forces 1941-46 and then resumed work on the ferry. He particularly missed Wick House and its stable (Broadwaters site today) just recently demolished for the old peoples' home, as the place too, settles down. For later details of Wick and its riverside, see The Last Village on the Dorset Stour, 1989.

MUDEFORD   6

The tiny village situated at the beautiful harbour mouth was traditionally, and perhaps most of all, a site for smugglers and fishermen having attracted, very early on, something of a Dutch colony and 'feel'. The Haven House and the Black House opposite are said to date from c.1600 and certainly, a small but picturesque collection of dwellings existed by the time the place was fought over in the famous and furious smuggling battle of July 1784 - such open defiance of the established powers abating somewhat after 1795 with the opening of Christchurch barracks. This new military presence locally now meant that control was slowly being extended over a previously wild region and, more firmly, with every addition to it, from 1812.

Moreover, as Christchurch (from their fine Bridge Street HQ) was the centre of a Preventive Service district (covering Calshot Spit to Handfast Point near Studland) and run by conscientious supervisors like Abraham Pike (c. 1803-4), so there began a slow movement away from the previous open lawlessness, sufficient perhaps to allow the first construction of the striking Georgian houses along this shore, these, of course, some way away from 'Mother Sellars' still notorious Ship in Distress Inn and its, so useful, channel near 'Standpitt'. Soon too, the Haven House was commandeered as a preventive station (1823) and it continued as such until at least 1857 when the coastguards moved their base to the 'western shore' (Southbourne), consequent upon the ending of the lease at Avonmouth. Small lookouts, however, were not relinquished as even the old boat at Steamer Point (c.1842+) was utilised, meaning that, in this way, all inner and outer approaches continued very well supervised and surveyed, subtlety and night runs being now more and more the key, instead of the old style open landings.

But now, it seems, additional, more legitimate activities were also coming (temporarily) to the fore, considerable shipbuilding taking place - the yards making sizeable vessels (of 200-250 tons) at and around the Black House even if, within its fabric, secret cupboards and hides remained very well known to the few. Here as well, John Bemister (later of Christchurch Quay fame) had a boat house and was much involved in this local industry before the business and this site generally was destroyed by the massive irruptions of sand caused by the disturbances of the iron workings - burrowing away on the nearby crumbling Head from 1848.

And all this disturbed local worthies and substantial landowners like George Henry Rose (at Sandhills, built 1785), W. Stewart Rose at Gundimore and their hopes for this 'newly discovered' retreat, complete with nearby romantic walks, wrecks and views - all in a place always a little out of time and strangely continental, the early Victorian letter box notwithstanding - these, not just local, celebrities perhaps attempting to keep it so. Whatever, as the following diary reveals, the covert was increasingly king hereabouts (as elsewhere, generally, in Poole Bay) even as a last smuggling venture (old style) dates to at least 1881 (cf. Oakley). Accordingly perhaps, it should be remembered, and most of all, that despite the swamping of this shore today by an almost endless suburbia, this belies the fact of its lonely, foreign, and decidedly other origin, blighted later, by the ironstone mines.

THE ROSE FAMILY

The Rose family interestingly, should not be neglected hereabouts for Sir George Rose (1744-1818), MP for Christchurch 1790-1812, was a key national figure. Secretary to the Treasury, friend of Nelson and advisor to George III, he played a key part in helping Pitt and the country recover from the loss of the American colonies. His earlier friendship with Arthur Phillip is also most noteworthy for he may have been instrumental in appointing Phillip as Commander of the First Fleet for Australia (1787-8), the connection being signalled by Rose Bay, just inside Sydney Heads and Rose Hill at Parramatta. So Mudeford is, it seems, linked with both early American and Australian history, the Rose family using it as a Summer retreat from both London and the family farm near Lyndhurst (where Phillip had been a neighbour). The 2 sons had their homes at Mudeford, side by side, Sandhills and Gundimore (including the Persian tent), and their presence goes a long way to explain the celebrity of all the guests connected with the early days of the little resort. The 'high society' ethos seems to have lasted a long time into the 19thC also, for the Roses were involved, as substantial local Avon Valley landowners, in the Christchurch Railway (1859+) and with the world of high finance around this mid century (see 1870 entry below re. G.B. Towsend).

EARLY MUDEFORD

c.1803-1815   After George III makes a fleeting visit en route for Weymouth and because France is closed off - a local dipping lady called Jane West begins the process of sea bathing at, hopefully, soon to be ultra fashionable, Mudeford (Muddyford). However, on moonless nights - much smuggling activity continues - the antidote to farming or boredom. The bar now begins to move north rapidly; some 100 yards, to 1836.

1823	The Haven House - a smugglers den - is commandeered as a Preventive Station. A Naval lieutenant and 10 men will be stationed here and it will continue in use to c.1857.
1836	J.H. Junkin is the Agent to Sir G.H. Rose of Sandhills, Mudeford: (MP for Christchurch).
1842-48	Boat building is carried on around the old Black House (c.1600) on Mudeford Spit. John Bemister has a boathouse nearby.
1848-49	It is recalled, as the first drifting sand begins to clog the harbour entrance, how in the time of Armstrong's and then Sylvester's, 1836 schemes for improvements - the average height over the bar at high water was 9'3" on an average tide of 5'6". There was a threat to the Salmon fishery. Other problem areas were shoals inside the harbour, viz. at Friskey or Mother Sellars' shoal (6'), Grandbarrow (5'8"), Smugglers Ditch (8'2¼"), and Claypool (8'5").

Also the area immediately below the confluence of the Avon and Stour produced something like a bar whereas many other parts of the harbour were deeper than 10' at high water.

Key stages in Christchurch Harbour (and so used as the annual Regatta route) were Swinney, Branders Bank and the Quay.

MUDEFORD IN 1850

The O.S. map for this period shows only about a dozen houses scattered near Mudeford, together with a few fishermens' cottages at the Haven. The settlement, the Georgian white houses notwithstanding, could only just compete with Wick for size. Empty fields and scattered farms otherwise. These were the halcyon special days, marked by flashes of Summer's sparkling blue. An age essentially, of elegant and aristocratic isolation. From 1850-1855, however, the depredations of the Warren Head ironstone mining increased, causing much protest (see Ironstone Canyon) and, some said, the death of Sir George Henry Rose on 17.6.1855. He is buried in the graveyard of Christchurch Priory.

July 1856	Lodgings and house accommodation are now reported "very scanty" at Mudeford since the Sandford Hotel "has gone". Locals urge a building movement. Meanwhile, the local cricket club (with 2 grounds) continues to meet at the hotel.
September 1856	Mudeford Regatta - the continuance of a tradition.

May 1857	Many feel Mudeford could become an important bathing place especially if the Christchurch Railway comes.
June 1857	Some bathers do not use Machines at Mudeford: "a disgraceful practice"!
August 1857	Others consider Mudeford to be too crowded in Summer.
January 1858	On Thursday morning (8th) a bunch of ripe red raspberries was gathered from Mr. Welch's garden at Sandhills, Mudeford. The flavour was said to be excellent.
June 1858	The artillery stationed at Christchurch barracks "again exhibited some excellent practice at Mudeford beach" using a 1,000 yard target flag barrel. They repeated the performance in October.
February 1859	G.F. Berkeley, writing in The Field, reports how "off the Christchurch Ledge, you can catch skate, fiddle and Monk fish and a sort of spotted shark called a nurse fish and huge conger eels."
June 1859	John Clarke of the Haven House pub (Mudeford) was charged with keeping open for beer sales between 3 and 5 p.m. on 15th May 1859. Fined 10/-.
October 1859	Pieces of Bournemouth's Pier are swept to Mudeford in a gale.
June 1860	Brook Cottage, Mudeford: to let. Apply J. Brown.
August 1860	Mudeford Sunday School outing.
June 1863	Newlyn (of Christchurch) puts on a 'bus' to Mudeford in the mornings, "for early dips".
August 1863	Mudeford cricket team play at their ground "near the quay".
September 1863	Mudeford Regatta continues successful.
July 1864	Local Mackerel Fishery. Several thousand fish were reported taken by one boat, though the shoal soon departed.
September 1864	The annual holiday of the fishermen of Mudeford and Stanpit (20-th); boat races &c. The Regatta this year is held on the 26th.
June 1867	A young lady is drowned in an accident at Mudeford.
May 1868	As sea bathing increases in popularity, there is an appalling accident at Mudeford (Wed. 20th May). 8 young men with a German tutor were bathing when there was a sudden surge of water. 6 of the boys were drowned and later one more was found dead. 2 were the sons of

Frederick Moser of Carbery House, Christchurch. Ages 13-15. The funeral provokes strong local editorials and feeling.

June 1868 More bathing machines are placed at Mudeford. Apparently the new bathing company had selected "an excellent new bathing ground" i.e. across the river mouth and on the spit - hopefully at some distance from the dangers of the Run.

September 1868 Like the rowing competition of the fishermen (July), the Regatta continues on schedule.

October 1868 The wreck of a lobster fishing boat off Mudeford. Two are drowned. This incident (6th) provokes a letter to the press from George B. Townsend, of Mompesson House, Salisbury and, locally, Gundimore, Mudeford: a solicitor and railway Parliamentary Agent. (One of his daughters "kept a very fully diary" of events.)

May 1869 Lord & Lady Bury are soon to take up residence at Mudeford.

June 1869 The School Chapel opens at Mudeford (Sunday 13th June). This was later to become All Saints Church. Architect J.L. Pearson. The Chapel was the gift of Mortimer Ricardo of Bure Homage - the local mansion. (There was a £1,000 endowment in 1876). Originally the Chapel served the small village community plus fishermen.

July 1870 Another young boy is drowned at Mudeford. The inquest is held at the Haven House Inn before J. Druitt Jnr., Deputy Coroner.

August 1870 G.B. Townsend dies on the shore below Gundimore on 29th August: "An eminent and well known solicitor" said the local paper but in fact a 'fixer' for many of the Contractors Lines, speculatively promoted, in the previous two decades, in and around Hampshire, Wiltshire and Dorset. This secret breed of men are only now being pursued and their work explored by modern social and economic historians.

May 1871 A small steam yacht goes aground on Christchurch Ledge - some remaining ironstone 'doggers' which once marked the shore line of the Head. However, although the erosion will continue unchecked for 68 more years, the Ironstone Mining Concession was now at an end. Meanwhile the sandbar at Mudeford continued to lengthen - almost to the line of Highcliffe Castle.

June 1871 Sandhills, Mudeford is for sale.

June 1872 A monster sturgeon (9'9") caught in the Run.

January 1873 Another 'Ship in Distress' inquest before Coroner, James Druitt. The evening school (built 1872) is now in process in the village whilst services continue at the Chapel.

September 1874	The annual treat of Mudeford School is held at Bure Homage.
July 1875	B. Battery, Royal Horse Artillery - have target practice at Mudeford - floating targets at 1500 yards.
July - Sept. 1877	Both cricket team and Regatta continue to prosper.
September 1880	Mudeford Chapel. First Harvest Festival (28th September). There is also a Mission Room in existence at Purewell.
December 1881	Storms block and then re-open the harbour entrance at Mudeford. This has been well removed by the drifting sands - to the East of the original Haven Run.
February 1882	A Sunday census (of 5th Feb) finds 147 at Mudeford Morning Chapel and 98 at the Purewell Mission Room that evening. The local population is now 213.
January 1884	Severe gales. The sea overflows the Sandbank.
February 1886	Another "sad and fatal" boat accident. Locally, the Sandbank has now stretched as far as Steamer Point. In time a lagoon will form behind it.
February 1887	A New Village Mission Room opens at Stanpit.
February 1888	A local recreation park for Stanpit is suggested.
January 1890	Soon the recreation ground is "completing".
March 1890	Churchgoers to Christchurch Priory, from Mudeford, travel there by boat.
April 1890	A 'Run' fisherman is said to earn 30/- p.w. approx.
September 1890	A fine Osprey is shot at Mudeford (29th).
December 1892	The Run fishery at Mudeford is said to be "extinct".
December 1896	Death of Col. Hudson of Mudeford.
May 1897	The Bere-Pan (Beerpans) is said to mean a Fish Pond, something - certainly indicated by its shape, off the Head and the good catches there.
January 1898	Christmas Day at Mudeford Church - two services.
January 1899	John Aird MP, Contractor for Irrigation works at Assouan (Aswan) and Sir Benjamin Baker C.E. visit the district.

Avon Run, Mudeford, Christchurch

MALLETT, PHOTO

Harbour View, Mudeford, Christchurch.

CM 345 The Barge Tea Boat, Mudeford.

COSENS & COMPANY'S PLEASURE STEAMERS

S.S. "Brodick Castle" off Christchurch Head.

The 'MARGARET' House Boat
HENGISTBURY HEAD

June 1901	Another drowning fatality at Mudeford.
March 1902	A boat accident at Mudeford. Lucky escapes. Salmon netting continues in the Run.
August 1902	The Royal Yacht is sighted in Christchurch Bay. The 'Victoria & Albert'.
September 1902	Salmon fishing in Christchurch bay - off Mudeford.
August 1903	A sad drowning case. A soldier at the Hengistbury Head Summer camp, rowing near Mudeford, is drowned. He had hired the boat from J.C. Edmonds at Wick Ferry.
December 1904	The Sandbank at Mudeford continues to grow as the erosion of the Headland remains unchecked. Not only is the spit lengthening towards Highcliffe Castle but a large swirl has developed just inside the Headland, by the spit's beginning.
1905-1910	Teaboats run in competition, at one or two piers inside Mudeford Spit.
June 1909	Military Sports are held at Mudeford.
July 1910	Another boating disaster at Hengistbury with 4 local people drowned.
Winter 1911	The long Sandbar is breached by a gale at the Run end but the lagoon remains. Sandhills 'destroyed' by fire in December. "Considerable damage" £5-6,000 worth, done.
May 1912	A plea is made to bring bathing at Mudeford under the control of the Council.
November 1916	Following the severe gale of the 5th - the sea walls at Sandhills (residence of Mrs. Wiggins) and Gundimore (Mrs. Surman) were badly damaged. The cottages at the Haven caught the full force of the gale and tide and were flooded. Mrs. Cutler and her three children who occupied the ground floor of one of the houses had to be rescued whilst Mrs. Cutler's 'Enterprise' refreshment rooms "were completely demolished by the waves."
1918	A sanctuary window is established in Mudeford Chapel. No guardship appears to have been stationed locally during the war.
January 1921	Avonmouth, Mudeford is for sale.
June 1921	The freakish changes "every few years" of the Sandbank are seen to be severely hampering the Harbour's future potential.

1924	Another breach in the sandbar occurs.
June 1926	Stunt flying is held at Mudeford Lane.
September 1930	A.J. Seal proposes a bridge at Mudeford - part of a grand marine drive.
Introduced in 1930's	The blessing of the Waters in the Run "for the harvest of the sea" is held on Rogation Sunday.
September 1931	Mudeford Chapel is dedicated to all Saints.
November 1931	Christchurch Council buy Avon beach.
April 1933	After F.C. Fisher's establishment of the local (Christchurch airport) Sir Alan Cobham's Air Circus arrives.
May 1934	Cobham's local air routes commence operations.
December 1934	There is a plan for a proposed aerodrome at Mudeford. Approved. (F.C. Fisher & H.C. Smith, partners.)
February 1935	On February 25th, the shingle bank at Mudeford, which stretched then for almost 2 miles to Highcliffe Castle, was broken through by the twin rivers during a heavy gale. Swiftly the water deepened the new cut at the Run (from 4 to 11 ft) and in 4 days the outlet was 50 yards wide making a much improved Harbour entrance.
	E.P. Hart (a Naval Architect from Poole) soon made a new chart of the configuration which, it was argued, should be consolidated by sinking 2 hulls filled with cement in the former course whilst a short groyne should be made on the seaward side to check drift.
March 1935	Blessing the Waters. Rev. E. Dixon presides whilst hundreds attend.
Summer 1935	Plans for the new Airport building at Christchurch (Mudeford) airport, reveal a fine Art Deco structure. It will never be built and rudimentary accommodation would continue.
July 1935	The Avon & Stour Catchment Board consider building a training bank 260 yds due east from the sea wall at Gundimore (for c. £4,590) but prefer the impending construction of the Hengistbury Groyne which it is thought, will push beach drift out into deeper water.
September 1935	On the 16th, there was a historic gale, 'said to be "the worst in living memory". It nearly 'islanded' the Haven Inn and the cottages at Mudeford, with only the little crumbling seawall, a riverside embankment, saving it all from being swept away. There was generally "severe encroachment" with over 100 yards of the Sandbank being lost.

This same month sees the formation of the Mudeford tennis club.

November 1935	More floods at Mudeford.
February 1936	Mudeford Quay is to be repaired. Nearly all its sea wall is either broken or crumbling. Messrs Devenish, who own the Haven Inn and adjacent cottages, plan a new concrete wall. The old wooden piles would be replaced by reinforced concrete using, if possible, local labour.
March 1936	Rev. Eric Dixon is filmed 'Blessing the Waters'. Meanwhile the new swifter running tides reduce the Salmon catch. Meantime, at Christchurch Aerodrome, Cobham's Air routes are extended. Several small companies now operate air connections here.
May 1936	Mudeford Quay repairs progress well - a London firm of contractors at work.
June 1936	The Lagoon (Mudeford Pool) still constitutes a risk to unsuspecting swimmers. Warning notices are to be posted. Redecoration of All Saints, Mudeford, goes ahead.
August 1936	There are said to be 400 beach huts now among the dunes at Mudeford, access helped by the new Broadway. Some are temporary Summer residences.
July 1937	There is a dispute over the private lease and access to the Mudeford Sandbank.
March - Sept. 1937	Discussions take place on the future of Mudeford beach. Additionally, there are serious cliff falls this year. Fears continue that Haven Quay will become an island. A landing stage is proposed for Mudeford Spit.
July 1938	Christchurch continues to develop its plans for Mudeford.
Summer 1939	The Air Speed Shadow factory - a large works to diversify Aircraft production - is established at Christchurch Aerodrome.
1940/1941	Special Duty Flight at Christchurch. For full details of this and the Fleet Air Arm Radar Unit 1942-46, see A. White Christchurch Airfield 1922-66, 1987 including a diary of operational details.
June 1944	Aircrash at Stanpit. (11 killed) 29th June. S.R.D.E. at Steamer Point: Nissen Huts and Radar.
July 1944	Mudeford Park Estate Bungalows are planned for Foxwood Avenue.
September 1944	2 soldiers are killed by an exploding mine at Mudeford.

November 1944	Official standing-down of the Home Guard.
1950+	A.J. Noott (Incumbent) Mudeford Church, revives the ceremony of blessing the waters for the harvest of the sea.
November 1954	Terrible storms take place (and in December) with big inroads by the sea. The Spit is breached seriously once again.

MUDEFORD SANDSPIT

Following the severe 60 m.p.h. gale of Sat. November 27th 1954, a review noted how the problems of the Sandspit dated to the depradations of the Hengistbury Head Mining Co.

The spit, it was said, had been breached and partly destroyed several times between 1880 and 1935 but in all cases the longshore drift of materials saw it grow again.

However, once the long groyne at Hengistbury was established (1937-9), this cut off the supply of sand with the result that, since then, the position of the harbour entrance had remained much the same.

E.B. Wise, Christchurch Borough Engineer

It was feared, therefore, that "unless permanent works were carried out", a breach of the dunes was imminent. The recent storm had seriously scoured into the dunes and destroyed beach huts.

December 1954	Mudeford Sandbanks must be saved! There are fears of a breach, following further gales on 25th/26th so threatening Christchurch. The Sandspit had been breached in 2 or 3 places - the sea rushing over into the harbour.
January 1955	Sea defence works take place following the great storm of 27.11.1954. The length of the Spit has now retreated to the Run - its once normal position.
February 1955	Mudeford sandbank problems continue. There are urgent pleas to save it and so avoid flooding in Christchurch.
December 1955	Christchurch remains worried about the condition of the Spit and make pleas to the Avon & Dorset River Board re protective works.
1957	Bure Homage House demolished - the key building of Mudeford.
April 1963	A Stanpit Nature Reserve Plan is set out.
May 1963	Lloyds Bank opens to serve the now fast growing 'village'
April 1965	Protests occur over the possibility of the Old Haven Inn at Mudeford Quay being demolished. It is argued that Mudeford has, "in recent

years, suffered an invasion of modernism in the form of bungalows and shops ... Cannot it now be left with what remains of the old village?"

June 1965	The 'Yard Birds' appear at the Bure Club, Mudeford.
October 1965	There is a rethink on 'flats'. Locals protest strongly about the increasing density.
November 1965	A Management plan for Stanpit Nature Reserve is almost completed. On 125 acres, there are over 200 different bird species.
January 1966	It is noted now how the Airfield at Somerford became Bournemouth Airfield under Sir Alan Cobham. Then nearby Hurn became Britain's transatlantic terminal 1945-6 before Heathrow opened. (Hard runway 1954)
May 1966	The annual blessing of the Waters (15.5.1966) continues.
April 1967	Mudeford prepares to tackle the oil from the Torrey Canyon spill. Cardboard boxes are assembled to transport the birds to the Sanctuary.
November 1967	A plan for a new dinghy base at Mudeford is proposed.
September 1968	Christchurch is attacked for allowing the growth of a 'shanty town' on Mudeford Spit. They hold a lease on it for 99 years.
October 1968	It is stated the Spit will be held by Christchurch until 2030. There are 212 private sleeping chalets and 64 owned by Christchurch Corporation. Rents are rising, however.
July 1969	Mudeford & Murder. Napoleon's Flotilla: A local mystery.
August 1969	A new local 'Run' record for salmon is set. 13 are landed in one net haul. 12 was the previous record in the 1930's (average 8 lbs).
October 1969	The Ship in Distress Inn (of Mother Sellar's fame) is said to date to 1670. It is the only pub of this name in the country and had once, a self contained brewery, with stables at the back for dray horses.
1973	Christchurch Council build a concrete seawall and other works on the Spit. Later the sand 'transfusions' in Bournemouth Bay will have positive effects on the barrier.
October 1976	The sea breaks through the Spit - into Christchurch Harbour and this despite the new coast protective works.
1978-1985	Extensive works continue on the Haven site.

December 1991	All Saints Church extension is opened by the former Bishop of Southampton, D. Cartwright (257 attend).
October 1992	New and expensive sea defence works and flood barriers are outlined for the Haven Inn peninsula - a response to global warming and the decay of the concrete piles.
Nov/Dec. 1992	A new porch is made for All Saints Church.

HIGHCLIFFE AND THE CASTLE

"Highcliffe Castle is the only house in England where the great Napoleon ever slept. And Napoleon never came to England. The explanation is that Highcliffe was originally the Chateau des Andelys, neiar Rouen, and was transferred bodily to Hampshire at the beginning of the last century."

1922 was the centenary of this now substantial place - once famously known as Slop Pond and then, Newtown, changing its latter name, at the request of the postal authorities, to one only a little more original later. Its development is really almost entirely modern however, save for the original villas of wealthy Victorians like Saulfland, Cranemoor, Latimers and Culmore plus Edwardian splendours best represented by E.S. Prior's magnificent Arts and Craft edifice, Greystones, now mercifully rescued from its near almost complete loss in the early 1970's. Survivor of many hurricanes, it seems always more real, on this furious shore, than any more fanciful construct - like the second Highcliffe Castle above.

But this latter was, in a way, the first out here on this woody, wilderness shore - a place, surprisingly, noted in Domesday as Sclive. John Stuart, Prime Minister, 3rd Earl of Bute built the precursor near these crumbling cliffs in 1770 whilst his grandson, Lord Charles Stuart de Rothesay, had the present building erected in the 1830's, incorporating the various French elements outlined. From this date too, comes Steamer Point (important in the Mudeford story) when this old vessel was towed here and beached for a summer house - a romantic sealodge set down in a virtual wilderness; long out of time and essentially 'foreign' in feel.

Thereafter, development, as elsewhere, seems to have been slow, St. Mark's Parish Church in 1843 and occasional extensions by Captain Hopkins, owner of the nearby Hubborn Estate, marking rudimentary first steps to a marine resort. It was all, one suspects, nicely secluded until the mainline railway swept by in 1888 to, once more, re-energize Bournemouth and send shock waves of new entrepreneurs all around. John Aird MP, civil engineering contractor, was one such, and we find him established at the Castle in January 1899 - the first of a number of prime movers of this now altered age. But still Royalty visited 1902-4 and, of course, most famously, the Kaiser in November - December 1907 - creating more than a little stir in this long unthreatened area. And as war came to Europe, Selfridge came to the Castle - in November 1916 - from which place, and most pertinent for this account, the complete redesign of Hengistbury was planned - Architect Tilden (see Appendix) revising and redrawing what was intended to be just the 'Largest House in the World' though we may see, as we look around the far humbler but more numerous estates today, how a kind of eventual democracy prevailed. Building sandcastles, it seems, is fun for everyone.

The local Salmon fishery has always been the quiet leitmotif of the harbour area even as the fishermen's interests and commercial affairs haunt the Victorian press accounts and of course, much of its local literature and memorabilia. There are even postcards, for example, showing them c.1905, busy not only at the Run, but even along the Wick shore where reed cutters had also been long active.

The 19thC. for them, nevertheless, was generally no easy time, particularly as more and more disturbance affected the key salmon pools of the twin rivers as did weed growth. Ironstone mining and the ever growing spit and harbour bar, perhaps most of all, impeded any easy access for the fish, through several seasons from the mid century, and not surprisingly therefore, the numbers caught fluctuated greatly - their chances of making it up river made still less by the types of net used.

But we are at least fortunate today to have a clear idea of the numbers of fish taken from 1814 onwards (see below) the dip coming , nor surprisingly, most around the mid century and continuing at a low level to c.1879/80, but blamed then on a number of causes (cf. N. Bell 1916) and not just the sand.

The subsequent removal of weirs &c. seems to have helped (and may be of river weed too) so that, by the 1880's, figures were again very encouraging - until another slump came at the end of the decade leading to fears of the extinction of the fishery at the Run (c.1892). But then Knapp Mill was destroyed by fire (Dec. 1898) and catches recovered (a $47^{3}/4$ pounder in 1905) so that, by 1913, 943 Salmon were again taken in the Run and 378 in the Royalty Fishery, weighing an average of 16 lbs (not to mention Pike, Perch, Chub and Roach).These improvements had been achieved by more and more controls of the Rivers and by licensing (hence the statistics) and the employment of Water Bailiffs like Henry Stride (for Lord Wimborne) who patrolled from Wick Ferry to Blackwater on the Stour and who caught poachers regularly off Tuckton Lane. Benjamin Pond too, was a riverkeeper when poaching was rife. C.1912-20 and he patrolled from Tuckton Bridge to Canford. By 1920 however, he began to note how both pollution of the Stour and dredging activity was combining to ruin the salmon holes with the result the numbers taken would inevitably be lower. Nevertheless, in season, up until the first war, Brown & Wilkes shop in Old Christchurch Road regularly had 6 or more local salmon "on the slab" - their heaviest ever fish being 56 lbs. The British record is 64 lbs caught by a Miss Ballantine, and the heaviest by fly, 'Tiny' Morison's 61 lb fish.

Apparently the bigger fish preferred the less troubled Avon and the others the Stour with Rod catches then, up to 400 and 50 in the Stour.

However, in the harbour today, the wild Salmon is now seen as "one of the Avon's increasingly rare visitors." The ancient custom of netting at Mudeford (which in August 1969 saw a 'record' net haul of 13 fish of 8 lbs average) having almost died out. Indeed local fishermen now do not bother to operate their nets for the first few months of the season. Thus in 1992, the first, a 13 lb specimen, was not caught until June (1st Feb. used to be the start of the season). John Batchelor, a leading Mudeford fisherman blamed overfishing in their migratory feeding grounds off Greenland and increased pollution of the Avon although Lord Normanton at Somerley could still report the Avon to be "quite a good Salmon river". A 30 lb fish (priced today at c.£9 per lb) he considered a great catch whilst many anglers still come and get good 20 lb Spring Salmon.

In 1601, the Salmon Fishery was worth £100 p.a. and c.£1,000 p.a. by the 18th C.

C.1836, Sir George Rose of Mudehaven gave the Fishing Rights to the Run Fishermen, viz. Abraham Cokes, George Stride, Henry Clarke and George Derham, which rights they utilized for several generations subsequently.

The following catches something of the more dramatic years.

In the late enquiry (1860) made at Ringwood by the Government Commissioners into the condition of the rivers Avon and Stour, the following evidence was given:

First, details of fish taken to that time, were:

1814	1,112	(1600 in the Royalty Fishery)
1815	1,551	
1816	1,160	
1817	502	(all net and rod)

but followed by a recent serious decline to just 68 fish in 1860, no doubt the occasion for the report.

The Avon was 67 miles long with a catchment basin of 166 square miles. It has once been navigable up to Salisbury c.1500-1735, fish weirs being banned from Henry VIII's time. A River Avon Navigation Act dates to 1664 and it involved much improvement and cutting being made - as still visible near Sopley. Yarranton's harbour schemes sought to build on this though the navigation continued viable for only some 40 years thereafter - effectively coming to an end when the new Long Rocks entrance was blocked in 1730. Thereafter, beach drift began to affect the fishery whilst by 1916, Nancy Bell could note "boating is much more difficult in the Avon than the Stour" on account of the reeds but, "in spite of all the drawbacks, a skilful and patient canoeist can make his way up past Winkton, Sopley and Ringwood."

As the Commissions were told (in December 1860),

"Salmon were taken by the net and rod. The Royalty extended for about 3 miles up from Christchurch Quay. The tide flowed up to Christchurch Bridge. Fishermen caught about half their fish above, and half below the bridge. They fished with draught nets, and used them in the Royalty. Thomas Hibberd, keeper and manager of the club water at Christchurch (which began at the mouth of the river) attributed the falling off in the Salmon in a great measure to the alteration in the course of the mouth of the river, as several old fishermen had informed him that formerly it used to run nearly straight out. There was a weir and eel stage at Winkton with an aperture a foot square for the fish to through as the law required. There was the Knapp Weir, about a mile and a half above Christchurch, it was a mill and they were allowed by Act of Parliament to put in racks to keep the fish back. They took them below with draught nets or by the rod. The racks were closed the whole of the week excepting from 4 o'clock on Saturday 'til 4 o'clock on Sunday, but there was a footsquare open from January to January. Some years ago there had been quite 100 fish above the weir. If the water was high, the fish went up more. The weir effectually kept the fish down, and they could not pass up the river unless through this foot square till the racks were pulled up. There was another weir at Winkton. There was a right, about a mile and a half from the mouth of the river, for a choul net, which was completely fixed by anchors and did not rise and fall with the tide. He fished for salmon with a trammel net. The River was under the Act of Anne. Winkton weir was about 2 and a half miles above the Knapp weir. It was not a mill weir, but entirely a fishing weir. The fish could only get up except through the foot square from 4 o'clock on Saturday, 'til 4 o'clock on Sunday. The eel stages could not kill them going up but he had heard that at the weir at Ringwood mill there had been a great destruction of the Salmon fry coming down. He had been told that they had been caught at Ringwood, and sold by the bushel basketfull at a time. He began to fish on the 1st of January and might get one fish in January, and 3 or 4 in February. They were in very good condition then. He had had them as heavy as 42 lbs but as they got them now they varied from 25 lbs to 36 lbs. Their principal fishing now was in May, June and July, when the fish varied from 9 to 20 lbs. They got Salmon peel in July and August. They also got bouge, and in some seasons a great quantity, but they had very much fallen off. All kinds of white fish had very much fallen off within the last few years.

Hibberd, in continuation, said that a gashouse had been erected at Christchurch within the last few years, but, though he had gone round it, he could not see that any fish issued forth. Fish began to fail about the 12th August, which used to be the beginning of the close time. The great proportion of the fish got heavy in spawn at that time. The club engaged the river; they angled at a certain time, and netted when they thought proper. They did not angle after the close time. The angling season was from February till the first fortnight in June: there were not many fish caught after that with the fly. He always saw that the foot square was kept open all year round. A steam tug had come into the mouth of the river during the last 5 years and that might have prevented the increase in the Salmon. (Note: The steamer 'Carrs' was used for the ironstone extraction from Hengistbury.)

John Mills Esq. of Bisterne, said he had been a fisherman all his life. He knew Christchurch, which had a bar harbour, and like all bar harbours, it was exceedingly shifting. The mouth of the river changed very frequently. At high water there was, generally speaking, only 8 feet there. The mouth of the river altered so much that when he went there occasionally he hardly knew where he was but he did not think that had anything to do with the decrease of the Salmon. Sir George Rose originally held the Royalty, and when the fishermen fished within it, he winked at it for a long time, and permitted them to do so, as they were his constituents in the borough of Christchurch and the result was that when, at length, a lawsuit was commenced they tried from usage to establish a right."

Christchurch Times
Sat. December 15th and 22nd, 1860.

From the remainder of the evidence before the Commissioners:

Frederick Derham said he knew the mouth of the river at Christchurch, and the net which was used there. They used it a mile from the harbour's mouth. It was a 6 inch mesh, and extended from the shore. It was a 6" mesh on the stretch. The net was not in use for a number of years until within the last 3 years, but he could recollect it as long as he could remember and his father used it before he was born. The right of using this net belonged to the Lord of the

Manor. It was not used for a number of years, as the gentleman did not reside at Somerford, but within the last 3 years it had been used again. He got one Salmon last season, and as in the rough weather he lost the net, he did not think that another would be got, as it would not pay. Formerly they used to catch a great many, from 15 to 16 a day. He attributed the falling off in the Salmon to the hatches and the gratings they put in at the weirs, as they stopped the fish from going up. The inhabitants of Christchurch considered they had a right to fish in the harbour and they exercised it up to this time. He had known a great many Salmon taken there. He had himself helped to catch 4 or 5 in one day. He had known as many as 16 boats fishing there.

Christchurch Times, Sat. 29.12.1860

Note: following the 1860 enquiry - the various Salmon impedences in the Avon continued to be a problem and for the Avon Salmon Fishery Association. In the Stour meanwhile, it was noted how the dense weeds kept the Salmon out, even more than the Avon, with the result that, for example, Tuckton's Mill, Hurn, was somewhat 'fish less', "beautiful but weedy" (see CT 16.7.1864). Occasional drownings - as at Knapp Mill - in August 1864 also served as a continuing reminder of the river's darker nature. The Earl of Malmesbury, however, did see the Stour's potential as a Salmon river detailing this in May 1865 with G.P. Mansel, Secretary to the Mudeford & Christchurch Fishermen continuing in much the same vein in February 1867 - the recent drop in 'takes' perhaps beginning to focus minds and on more licensing controls. So it was reported, draft nets needed a licence "if used in the Run" (July 1867) whilst you had to have a licence as an individual "to fish either the Avon or Stour" (February 1868).

These details apart, however, blockages and obstructions appeared to be the real problem - as an Inspector of Salmon Fisheries reported on 26th-27th March 1868. Hindrances to fishing included, he said, the traditional activities in the Run but also the numerous weirs. However, re the former it was deemed "practically impossible to interfere with the fishermen in the Run" as fishing rights were common there. Thus although it was considered a "particularly destructive fishery" little could be done. So, as it was "not practicable" to interfere with the Run fishery, the recommendation was rather "they do away with the fatal weirs" and also "erect Salmon ladders."

Christchurch Times, 11.4.1868

The weeds meanwhile, continued a major problem, with, even in 1870, "scarcely a Salmon to be found in the Stour." The reason being "about 200 yards up the Stour from its confluence with the Avon, the river was said to be "completely blocked with rushes and river weeds, so that after March it was almost impossible for a fish to pass them, whilst just beyond on either side was swift and deep water." As a proof that fish would ascend the Stour, several were noted to have passed up during February and March before the weeds and rushes had commenced to vegetate." The river silted up at the reeds - hence the ford at Wick (which marked the frontier).

In Summer, the water "just trickled through a forest of bulrushes and water hemlock." Just below the reed barrier "was one of the best holes in the district (Swinney) - a place where Salmon congregated in great numbers."

The Field, April 1870

The Avon Salmon catch in 1870 was:-

With the net (Run)	652
Knapp	1300
Winkton	60
Aldridge	12
Fane	10
Bistern	34
	2068

Average weight: 11 lbs

Christchurch Times, 28.5.1870

1871-1890

As may be seen from the statistics below, however, - the good year of 1870 notwithstanding - Salmon catches did not rise to 4 figures again until the mid 1880's by which time we can guess the disturbances from the ironstone excavations and to the coast were beginning to stabilize somewhat.

In 1871, the Salmon Fishery in the Run began on Monday 6th March whilst rod and line takes were recorded at Ringwood (32 lbs, 41") in February 1875. A record haul of 14 on one net is said to date to June 1875.

Statistics for 1884 seem to have been encouraging enough and for the Christchurch paper to record them weekly from 29.3.1884; viz 52 being taken in the Run to the 27th, 84 in the Run 8-15th May; and 75 (Run) 5-12th June etc. though in the Royalty Fishery "the weeks take (12-19th June) did not exceed half a dozen." These good years saw the newspaper continue its diary of catches to 1886 but when the slump came - so it desisted, another Salmon Fishery enquiry being instituted from August 1888. Despite this however, a Run Fisherman earned approximately 30/- p.w. in 1890 even though just 19 Salmon were caught there at the start of that season.

Report on the Salmon Fishery in 1890

"In the Estuary called the "Run" - is a public fishery, the area of which is about 200 yards long by 60 yards across. The 'Royalty' fishery, situate in the Avon, is private, and belongs to Mr. Mills whose fishermen catch a large number of Salmon. The flavour and colour of a fresh run Christchurch Salmon is well known to fish lovers all over the Kingdom, and cannot be surpassed, probably not equalled, by the Salmon of any other river. Early in the season it is sold at 2/9d or 3/- a pound, sometimes more but afterwards sells as low as 16d. In the season of 1875, the first 2 fish caught sold at 5/- per pound. Before the passing of the Salmon Acts (1861-1873) there was no restriction whatever upon the public fishery. In recent years, however, the time of fishing has been curtailed, and a heavy licence, with other restrictions, has been placed upon each net. There is a Board of Conservators for the Avon and Stour fishery district (elected by the County authorities of Hants, Wilts and Dorset) which has power to enforce bye-laws for the conduct of all kinds of fishing within the district. Since 1875, the public right of fishing has extended from the 2nd February to the 14th August in each year and the season for rod and line fishing has annually extended from the 2nd February until the 1st of October. The dates of the season have often been a source of controversy between the fishermen in the public waters and the upper proprietors. The fishermen have desired to commence in January instead of in February, and close in July instead of in August but have been unsuccessful in their agitation. A new bye law was passed by the Conservators in Feb. 1891 to alter the net fishing season by taking off a fortnight at the end, thus making it to terminate on the 31st July instead of on the 13th August. The Christchurch Salmon run very large, especially early in the season.

The takes of Salmon vary very much. In 1886 there were 22 less nets at work in the 'Run' and 603 more fish caught than in the following year. Mr. John Mills once stated that when he was a boy, 53 Salmon were caught at Bisterne during one year and only 3 in the year following. During the past 22 years the total number of Salmon caught in the 'Run' was 12,894 - an average of 556 and a fraction a season. It was reported in 1888 that during the preceding 5 years the nets of the riparian owners of the Avon and Stour yielded 2,085 Salmon and that the average number caught in the 'Royalty' Waters was 640 annually. In 1886 there were caught:-

By the Nets

In the Run	1685 Salmon weighing	30,453 pounds
	39 Sea Trout "	156 "
In the Royalty	562 Salmon "	10,078 "
And by 95 rod licences	156 Salmon "	3,306 "
	2,442	43,993

The fishing during 1890 was very much below the average: it was pronounced 'a bad season'. In the Run, the takes had not been so small for 15 years. The following authentic statistics show the number of rods and nets used, and the total fish caught during the past 22 seasons.

| | No. of licences granted | | | No. of Fish | | Total/without Royalty |
	Net	Rod	Total	Run Nets	Caught at Run	
1869	19	11	30	...	652	768
1870	20	16	36	...	901	1060
1871	30	17	47	...	567	...
1872	20	18	38	...	376	450
1873	20	19	39	12	381	475
1874	18	20	38	9	276	378
1875	15	14	29	7	227	311
1876	21	24	55	12	431	604
1877	19	36	55	11	330	413
1878	20	43	63	14	318	393
1879	19	33	52	13	371	428
1880	17	23	40	11	661	766
1881	21	37	58	15	663	803
1882	30	77	107	24	842	...
1883	30	92	122	23	1435	1885
1884	33	85	118	26	1072	1515
1885	21	78	99	14	761	1089

1886	24	95	119	16	1443	...
1887	46	93	136	38	840	1687*
1888	28	79	99	20	557	878
1889	28	55	83	21	547	660
1890	27	70	97	20	243	321

* with Royalty

The heaviest Salmon ever caught in the "Run" weighed 52³/₄ lbs. This, a good conditioned male fish, was caught by S. Shambler on 2nd April 1880 and was sold to some admirers of Mr. J. Edwards Moss, a candidate in the local Parliamentary election then taking place. The fish measured 4' 4¹/₂" in length and 2'4" in girth. On Feb. 18th 1891 another fine male Salmon was caught by C. Harrison weighing 42 lbs and, on April 3rd 1891, J. Eyers caught a splendid fish weighing 44.¹/² lbs which measured 3'11" in length, 2'2" in girth.

The duty imposed by the Conservators on a draft net for Salmon is £3 while a rod licence for Salmon is £1. It is pretty generally believed that Christchurch Salmon was, at one time, more plentiful than it is today and there is a legendary story that indentures of apprenticeship had a clause that the boys, during their apprenticeship, should not have Salmon given them to eat more than so many times a week: Warner says that when he was a schoolboy he saw 95 salmon taken at a draft at Claypool and that the net revenue from the fishery was £1,000 a year.

Christchurch Times, 18.4.1891 (Sat)

Note: The Stour Fishery Club preserved the River from the Sheep Wash (Near Iford Bridge) to Wick Ferry. Weekly tickets 10/-: day ticket 3/6 or 5/- for Salmon.

Christchurch Times, 27.9.1890

The Avon & Stour Fishery suggested increasing their area of Jurisdiction in May 1906. By this date, Salmon fishing had "greatly decreased" - a great falling off meant that there were "practically none caught at all.

SALMON IN THE 20thC

Catches recorded:	1932	701
	1933	758
	1934	1,413
	1935	959
	1936	404

1935 was an unremarkable year at the Run, partly by contrast with the previous season which saw the biggest catch for close on half a century. The record year was 1886 when 1,443 fish were taken.

1936 saw a disastrous Salmon fishing season - "one of the worst in living memory" C.J. Galpin, Water Bailiff, blamed the decline on recent changes in the Run following the new break in the Spit. Now fishermen had to cast their nets by the Black House into what they called "wide water", a point where the Salmon could easily avoid the nets (in the February-July Season). The Sandbank had not built up at all since the breach at the Run and it was thought only 1 fish in 50 making the Run was ever caught in the nets. The order of fishing was still decided in the time honoured way of drawing lots.

It would surprise us today to see this landscape as it was just over a century ago. Then there were very few houses or farm buildings anywhere and only about an equal number of trees. Instead, a great swathe of heathland spread down from the hamlet on Pokesdown Hill, and gradually fell away to the twin rivers in the east. Hengistbury would be familiar, no doubt, if larger, the scattering of Wick, the farm at Tuckton and, of course, Christchurch and its Priory - the great centre for this complex shore. But there was very little else, save a small oak wood at Foxholes, the remnant of its fort, well worn smugglers routes and wildfowl 'flyways' over "fairly good agricultural land" - marked, where Compton later established his Southbourne resort, by locally numerous walls, deep set to keep out rabbits and these for a number of well used pig sties.

Away to the West, meanwhile, Boscombe presented much the same clifftop wilderness, though maybe better protected and with many more fir trees. Financier Wolff had only just established himself there and, by encouraging land companies, was hopefully, serving to improve it, making a twin thereby for the 'marine village of Bourne'.

But Southbourne, in 1870, had just its new coastguard station, gun battery and, nearby, three small one storey cottages - one connected with farm buildings at Cellars Farm. Henry Scott, the occupant of that nearest the sea, was, in due course, to become the Bailiff to Dr. T.A. Compton during the period when he too decided its exposed and eroding shore seemed set fair for Victorian redevelopment. And with that decision, it seems, everything now changed, as a church, shops, Winter Garden, pier and hotel all appeared in short order to rapidly part urbanize and disorient this ancient place. So was a dream to be half realised and long before Selfridge thought he could do much the same on nearby Warren though both would discover money, as much as the pounding Winter gales, would prove their major handicap - the main limiting factor.

Inland, meantime, there was already Stourcliffe House (and attendant farm) built by Wiltshireman Wadham Locke; this grand surviving mansion set in nearly 500 acres - a forgotten surrounded pearl now on this tableland, though setting the stately tone. Bournemouth architect Creeke, at one time, was its intended land improver. This eyrie mirrored also Carbery House not far away and the, even then, famous Avonmouth at Mudeford or Sloman's elegant Wick House by the riverside - this latter providing the counterpoint. Altogether they formed an attractive and unusual group, little 'oases' within the enveloping heather where, otherwise, just lonely inns, like the forgotten Heathpoult, served the, usually very few, local travellers and smallholders active here. But alas even at that time the whole plateau was obviously - site for 'much needed' improvement whilst, unlike central Bournemouth, there was it appears, no one really large enough landowner present to really fully protect it as happened with Hengistbury and further west. So was to be sealed its speculative future and no longer perhaps, a quite so extraordinary fate though it is a bizarre transformation for all that. What follows captures something of the process.

1849   Wadham Locke (of Seend Nr. Devizes - like 'smuggler' Trotman) buys 485 acres including 2 miles of seafront at and around Stourcliffe House - which he has built. On leaving the place in 1857, C.C. Creeke was engaged to lay it out for marine villas - although Locke's daughter (married to Captain William Lamb) continued to live locally and for the rest of her life.

1867   Frederick Moser, a director of the Ringwood-Christchurch Railway Co. is established at Carbery House. Prior to this Moser was at Avonmouth House whilst Solicitor G.B. Townsend (see entry) was at nearby Gundimore.

By this date, Henry J. Smith was the owner of Stourcliffe and it was his son, Charles Edmond Smith, who was remembered by the broken column monument placed on Double Dykes following the gun accident in 1861.

1870   Dr. T.A. Compton buys a considerable amount of the cliff and foreshore from General Cleaveland - the owner since 1865. Also a narrow strip of land running to Tuckton from John Sloman at Wick House - this latter to give access to his now named Southbourne on Sea Estate (230 Acres total). It was, said Compton, bordered on the West by a smuggler's track, on the North by Heatherlea and Stourcliffe Houses, and on the East by Hengistbury Head, the property of Sir George Meyrick. At this time the only 'roads' on it were two small lanes, both of which led to Wick and also Tuckton lane. The first house to be built on the cliff would be called Sandycote...set among 'coveys of partridges'. Land sales began in July 1871.

1871   The only outside link, other than Wick Ferry was via the Old Iford Bridge and the first work necessary therefore, was to dramatically improve access. So Belle Vue Road was made and planted with firs - leading down to the intended first Tuckton Bridge (Act 1881). In the early 1870's land near Guildhill Road nearly became the site of a unique TB Institute to a Russian plan involving cows breath ventilation. Only a few firs were planted, however.

1871-78   This is the period of the establishment of the resort - well covered in Compton's own words, in Southbourne's Infancy 1918. The very special climate of the tableland, its good drainage and openness of aspect soon encouraged speculative building (of very substantial villas) e.g. Foxholes, Miramar, Sandycote, the Lodge.

By 1875 when Compton added Cellars Farm - with the population increasing and no church closer than the mother church of Pokesdown, St. James - so a small building for 100 was opened by a private individual (in 1876), and used as a Church school during the week. The name of St. Catherine's was chosen by deft comparison with St. Catherine's Hill and the point on the Isle of Wight - a framing reference on the horizon.

In 1870 also, a Winter Garden was established as a first tourist lure for developing Bournemouth's visitors to explore. On the beach, Trouville bathing boxes were another diversion for Summer ... though in Southbourne, not surprisingly, it was noted there were "very few lodging houses" for longer term visitors.

A visitor in Nov. 1876 observed "the Winter Gardens at Southbourne stands on "one of the bleakest portions of that pretty estate."

September 1879   The Poole & Dorset Herald reported:

"We believe we are correct in stating the place had neither road nor name ten years ago whilst only five years since not a single house had been built there."

Southbourne will now possess a Post Office in addition to a school, church and Winter Garden." (Beamish - first postmaster)

Note: The new P.O. (operated by the London Postal Authorities) was to have two daily deliveries. Only a bridge now was "much wanted" over the Stour - to link with Christchurch Station.

Spring 1882   Southbourne on Sea Freehold Land Co issues its prospectus and plan. This shows already existing houses like 'Spiekers' opposite the Winter Gardens, the Rocket Road to the beach, eastward of the coastguard station, down to the rocket post at the end of today's Harbour Road. Here was the Volunteer's practising battery. Map by Nash, Waters & Nash of Bournemouth. Land Auctions will continue to November.

Summer 1883   The works on the replacement St. Katharine's Church near completion, i.e. 2 bays for the nave and a new Chancel. Meanwhile the Undercliffe Parade is begun comprising 6 houses set on a promenade a third of a mile long and protected by an 8 ft seawall. It will be "nearly all wreck by 1914".

August 1884   A temporary transfer of the Southbourne Cliff Hotel licence is made from Mrs. Lamb - the present occupant, to Mr. & Mrs. McEwen Brown (Secretary of the Co.). Winter Garden Manager G. Ellen (1876+). Southbourne Farm - Mr. Scott : Coastguard Station, Mr. Richards. A subsidy of £100 p.a. was paid for a 2 horse bus running 3 times daily to Bournemouth.

October 1884   The Southbourne Pier plans are announced.

November 1884   A Visitor Notes: "A month or two since I had never heard its name: but in the search for some untrodden paths for our Autumn holiday we came through the New Forest to the Hampshire coast and there on the cliffs, a mile or two from Christchurch found a cluster of good houses, dotted here and there amongst the furze and bracken, where but a short time since was only a solitary coastguard station. In common with other places on this seaboard, Southbourne possesses a fine view of the

Channel. It has also the peculiar sandy soil and dry climate of the southern coast and on account of the mildness of the Winter, a good many residents have built houses, inland and on the cliff, but, wherever there is a waste piece of land, the bracken and sweet scented heather still thickly covers it. At present there are no streets and very few shops; no inn or cottages, workpeople have to come in from Christchurch; there is one good hotel, well situated in gardens; and the new church of St. Catharine has been completed this year."

Bournemouth Observer, 8.11.1884

September 1885	Sir Horace Davey - the local MP, opens the Undercliffe Parade.
November 1886	Consecration of St. Katharine's Church on Thursday 25th. Alfred Birt: Architect. Whigham is the first vicar followed by Messrs. Johnstone & Forse.
December 1886	Southbourne Parade houses - critics are replied to. The Undercliffe is felt - with the addition of a new pier - to be the key to Southbourne's success.
August 1888	Southbourne Pier is opened to visitors on the 6th (see separate entry below).
May 1891	Dr. & Mrs. Compton occupy No.4 of the 6 Undercliffe Villas with Mr. & Mrs. Butler in No's 5 and 6. 1-3 are empty.
Summer 1891	Bright's Guide notes the valuable Chalybeate Spring at Southbourne - now under the Promenade.
May 1892	The Stourfield Estate (above Tuckton) is bought by 'speculators'.
April 1894	More building sites along the clifftop are offered for sale. Meantime many girls schools will be set up in the area after this date, e.g. Grassendale, St. Cuthberts.
May 1895	Compton has now left his Undercliffe Home (for S. Devon) and only the Butlers remain. No other occupants and to 1898.
1898	Southbourne's Water tower is opened by the W. Hants Water Co. replacing the Iford Lane, Tuckton works of 1882.
February 1900	Completion of St. Katharine's Church. By April, the Parish area would be united within Bournemouth's new County Borough.
October 1900	A new sewage scheme is begun. Just as the first serious gales begin to destroy the seawall, pier and general dream.

June 1901	The bankrupt Southbourne on Sea Building Estate Co. offers further land for sale as it concludes.
Summer 1904	The 6 houses on the Undercliff Parade are demolished and their materials sold for salvage.
July 1905	Opening of St. Katharine's Parish Hall, Southbourne. Approximate period of the building of Church Road houses.
August 1905	The pier is said now to constitute a real danger on the sands.
February 1906	St. Katharine's National School. Misses Harwood and Olive Courtney - teachers.
Autumn 1910	Farmer Head continues at Cellar Farm to this date. Harbour Road will be known as Cellars Lane to 1930.
December 1916	Solent Road on the Cellars Farm Estate is reached by the erosion, following severe gales.
September 1921	A fishing boat overturns off Southbourne Kiosk - one man is drowned.
March 1923	The Wentworth area of cliff top at Boscombe is still a 'forest'.
February 1926	Southbourne & Pokesdown are deemed already joined together. Replanting is urged for Southbourne 'Grove'.
October 1933	Studland fatality. The body is washed up on Hengistbury Head.
January 1935	Various pieces in the local press appear on the development potential of the place.
July 1935	The Phenomenal building growth locally is noted in line with the vast growth in house building nationally. The home is now to be a consumer unit with services coming to it.
November 1935	W.E. Clowes is the new Borough Engineer.
July 1936	Arthur Bedford buys the beach front from Mr. Curling Hunter, liquidator for Rugbey Ltd £25,000.
December 1936	5000 tons of sand dunes are removed on the overcliff. St. Peters School is begun by Jesuits.
July 1937	Future of St. Peters School site: Vast schemes are envisaged.
W.W.2 1939-45	Defensive works, including several pill boxes, sprout along the shore. Bournemouth's bombing history begins at Cellars Farm Road, Southbourne on 3 July 1940.

January 1947	Coast erosion brings two cliff top pillboxes to Bedford beach. One remains here, upturned, until c.1970, the other incorporated in the sea defences.
February 1947	Overcliff gardens lost to erosion. The De La Salle Bros. take over at St. Peters.
May 1953	Southbourne coastguards practise.
March 1956	Arthur Bedford sells his beach to the Council, it changing hands after 20 years. Previous negotiations had taken several years. Fortes, the present renters of the cafe continue this year.
April 1956	New use for 'Canute Cafe'? which had been unused since 1939. This cafe, protected by steel plates was built in 1937 but was badly sited. It had not been used as a cafe since the war.

St. Katharine's Church, Southbourne - on - Sea
Sanl's Series.

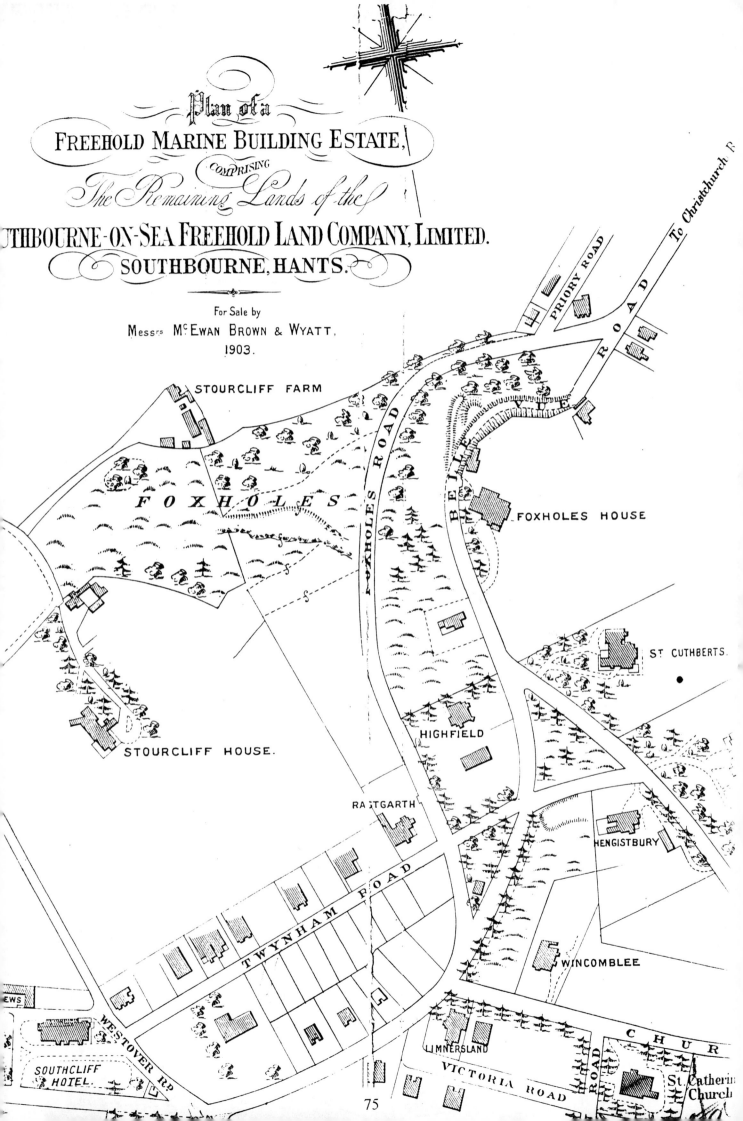

Plan of a
FREEHOLD MARINE BUILDING ESTATE,
COMPRISING
The Remaining Lands of the
UTHBOURNE-ON-SEA FREEHOLD LAND COMPANY, LIMITED.
SOUTHBOURNE, HANTS.

For Sale by
Messrs McEwan Brown & Wyatt,
1903.

To Christchurch R

PRIORY ROAD

ROAD

STOURCLIFF FARM

BELLE VUE

FOXHOLES

FOXHOLES ROAD

FOXHOLES HOUSE

ST CUTHBERTS.

STOURCLIFF HOUSE.

HIGHFIELD

RASTGARTH

HENGISTBURY

TWYNHAM ROAD

WINCOMBLEE

EWS

WESTOVER RD.

SOUTHCLIFF HOTEL

LIMNERSLAND

VICTORIA ROAD

CHUR

ROAD

St. Catherin
Church

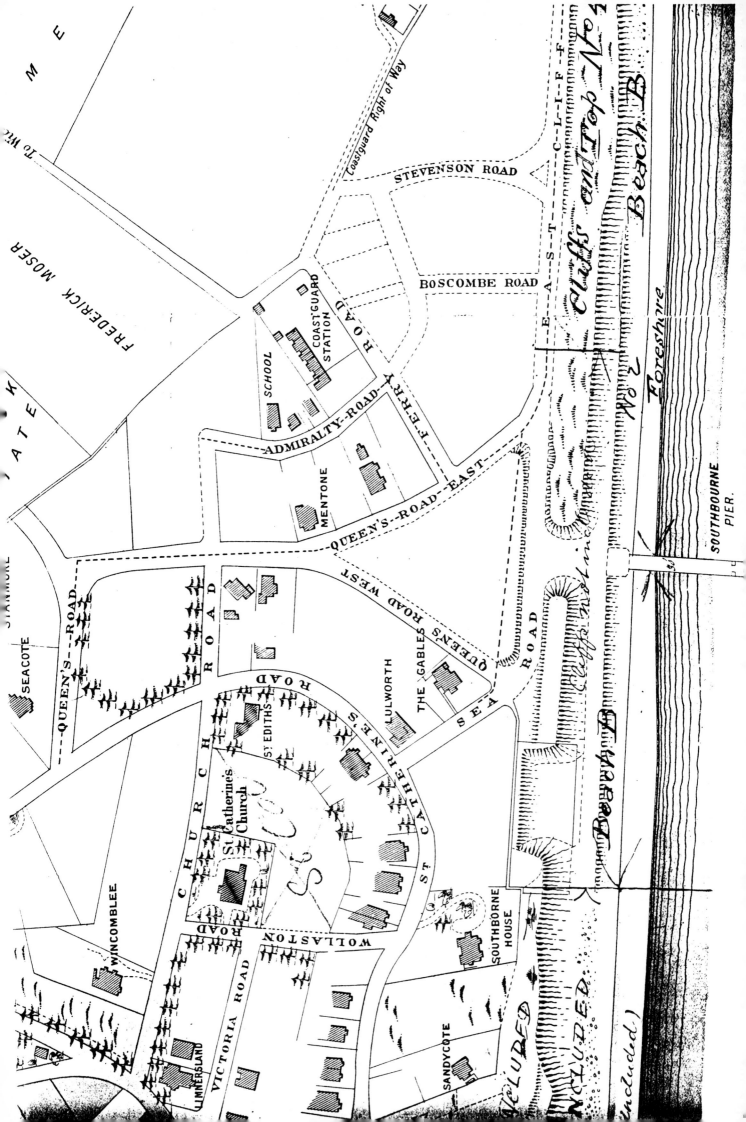

9

THE PIER AT SOUTHBOURNE: A PIER TO SHED

March 1885 — Proposed Pier at Southbourne approved by the Board of Trade - the new power concerning coastal matters. Messrs. Law & Chatterton (Engineers), Smith (Res. Engineer) under whom the sea-wall at Southbourne was built.

The estimated cost of the work was £6,500 for an iron pier and a shed and landing stage on the bed and foreshore of the sea. The pier was to project 800' into the sea with the deck 17 feet above High Water Mark. It was to 'combine ornamental surroundings with convenient arrangements for promenading."

September 1885 — Opening of Undercliff parade at Southbourne on Sea on Thursday 24th September.

October 1886 — The first steps to erect Southbourne Pier began this week.

August 1888 — Southbourne Pier was opened on Monday (6th) and nearly 1200 passed the turnstiles during the day. The Boscombe band played a fine selection of music, and the weather being fine, there were large numbers about the esplanade, cliffs and beach. The Lord Elgin steamboat called at the pier at 9 o'clock and took a considerable number of passengers on board for Bournemouth, but the sea being rather rough the Captain did not attempt a second visit and the large number of people who went on the pier for the two o'clock steamboat excursion had to be disappointed. The weather during the week has been on the whole very fine and the pier has consequently been largely patronized. It appears that the landing stage (although of the form suggested by the steamboat company and in the shape of a T) does not offer necessary accommodation for steamboats calling and the pier

The Sands from the Cliff

77

company have, we understand, given instructions for the required alteration to be made and the whole structure to be completed and ready again for calling within three weeks. Southbourne is now quite full of visitors and it seems a pity to debar them from the pleasure of the seatrip which the accomplishment of the pier would afford. The chief attraction of next week will be the bazaar at the Winter Gardens.

September 1888	The Bournemouth steamboat companies 'neglect' Southbourne Pier, so a fine steamboat 'belonging to Hastings' was hired and placed on the station (as from 3rd September). "The pier was patronized by upwards of 50 persons a day during the past fortnight, and the works connected with the lengthening of the structure are being rapidly pushed forward." The 'Nelson' timetable was widely advertised - i..e. running from Southbourne to Bournemouth and on 'pleasure trips'. Later it was stated; "The steamship 'Nelson' has come and gone. She spent only 2 days on the station, then had a 'slight accident.'
January 1890	The gale (on Thursday 23rd January) worked away part of the esplanade at Southbourne on Sea 'as well as the wooden breakwater at the Southern end of the wall. Large portions of the cliff foundered, with the sea (spray) even over the top of the cliff.
February 1892	The pier approach at Southbourne on Sea, badly, damaged in gales, is to be re-erected.
March 1894	The worst storm of the century takes place.
Nov. & Dec. 1898	Severe gales in the Channel on Wednesday 23rd November, the Bonne Mere (a French barque) with a captain and 12 men was driven on to Southbourne beach. The Ernst of Barth (North Germany) was wrecked off the Needles - a raft drifting to Warren Head.
December 1898	The Marie Therese, 3 master (c. 500 tons) driven on shore at Warren (Tues. 27th).
March 1899	On Friday afternoon (3rd), there was a sale by auction, at Hengistbury Head, of the cargo of the Marie Therese. The wreck was sold for £40 to a syndicate of Christchurch businessmen led by Bemister. The wreck was later partly destroyed by the military as part of a training exercise although (on picture evidence) it was to be several years before the whole wreck disintegrated.
Winter 1899/1900	The Southbourne Pier supports nearest the promenade are washed away in a severe gale.
December 1900	More gale damage occurs to the now derelict pier.
January 1901	The remnants of Southbourne Pier become the subject henceforth of photographers and post card publishers who graphically chart its decay.

The Beach, Southbourne

SIDNEY HOUSE,
OVERCLIFF DRIVE, SOUTHBOURNE-ON-SEA.

April 1901	Death of J.E. Holloway: Meanwhile the Southbourne Land and other Co's cannot find the funds to restore either the pier or derelict promenade. Compton argued a 'step' in front of the vertical wall would have saved it all.
Summer 1907	The remains of Southbourne Pier are still a lure, one reason being there is easy beach access here.
February 1908	Another great gale (on Sat. 22nd) almost removes all remaining trace.
January 1909	The old pier wreck continues to defy the waves. Observers admire its toughness but request demolition.,
January 1933	Last remnant of the pier, Canute's Chair', tumbles and only the rocks remain.

10

TUCKTON BRIDGE COMPANY

November 1880

"Alarmists have circulated a rumour that when the Tuckton bridge is completed, no-one will be allowed to go over the river at Wick. This is, of course, a fiction. It is said there used to be a ferry at Green Low Lane just where the bridge is to be and it is to lay the ghost of this ancient ferry that the promoters of the bridge insert the clause about ferries in their advertisements. No one has used this ferry for years, and no one wants to use it so its entire abolition will hurt nobody."

February 1881

The intended bridge, it is said, will not interfere with the now existing ferry at Wick (run by Mrs. Miller), William Crouch is the engineer of the undertaking and he estimated the cost as follows:-

Iron bridge 24' wide	£3,871
Approaches	£1,103
Toll House	£ 180
Contingencies	£ 515
Total	£5,669

Directors: J.E. Holloway, J. Druitt & Co (c30).

A free bridge was the ideal if enough finds could be subscribed - but many investors wanted a toll. Capital £6,000 in 600 x £10 shares.

May 1881

Promoters meeting. Compton, Col. Brander et al (on 5th). The Bridge Co. Directors are Dr. T.A. Compton (Chairman) (Teignmouth, S.Devon), Frank Moser (Carbery), James Druitt (Deputy Chairman). Col. W.M. Brander ('Spiekers', Southbourne), George Reeks (Wick-Hengistbury), William Tucker (Christchurch). Also J. Kemp Welch and J.E. Holloway.

Incorporated by the Tuckton Bridge Act 1881. Treasurer - Henry Stokes, Wilts & Dorset Bank, Christchurch. Secretary - Robert Druitt, Christchurch. Offices: High Street, Christchurch.

May 1883

After Tenders were received in April 1882, the first Tuckton Bridge opened this May.

1888

Return from Tuckton Bridge Co.:

Traffic is
40 x 4 wheeled carriages
31 x 2   "   "
6 x horses
6 x bicycles
110 x pedestrians
193 calves, sheep &c.

Receipts   16/¹/₂d   Signed G. Clark

Note: Southbourne Pier opened 6..8.1888.

January 1890	The tolls taken at Tuckton Bridge during the 26 weeks between July and December (1889) amounted to £169-2-4d. The shareholders receive a dividend for the half year, of 6% - "a higher rate than has yet been paid since the formation of the Co. in 1881".
May 1890	The tolls taken at Tuckton Bridge during the past 6 months averaged 18/7 per day. The capital of the Co. is raised by 410 shares issued at £10 each and held by 39 shareholders who have received a dividend for the past half year of 6%. The cost of the formation of the Co. and the construction of the bridge was £3,921-6-1d.
November 1896 & October 1897	Possible repairs to Wick Ford mooted: See entry.
December 1898	A visitor asks, "Who is responsible for the wretched 'home' provided for the tollkeeper (and his delicate wife) of the Tuckton bridge? Surely it is a disgrace to both directors and shareholders."
August 1901	Wick Ford - is thought practically impossible to maintain and repair.
June 1903	Sale of Wick Ferry (Mrs. Miller) by Ferry Auction. It did not reach its reserve price of £1,500 and was withdrawn.
March 1905	Extension tramway contracts let - for the 3 miles to Christchurch which would require a stronger Tuckton Bridge. Accordingly the contract was let to Messrs. J.G. White & Co Ltd (London) for £39,000. The hope was to complete by the end of July and the Christchurch part by the end of May.
	Tenders received from: a) Messrs Douglas & Richards; b) William Griffiths & Co; c) Ground & Newton; d) Dick, Kerr & Co. Ltd.; e) F. Osman; f) J.G. White & Co Ltd (Accepted) for the tramway extension. viz. 1) steel grooved girder rails; 2) permanent way construction and rail bending; 3) wood block and granite set edging.
	The hope was to get trams to Christchurch over Tuckton - Bridge - by August Bank Holiday.
May 1905	Overhead Equipment for new tramway by British Electric Equipment Co. £4,315 tender accepted.
September 1905	The new Tuckton bridge was to be ready in about a month, the tramway in 2-3 weeks "allowing for the concrete setting".

October 1905	Tramways: Opening of entire route. On Saturday morning (14th) 4 of the massive tram cars ran down to Tuckton bridge for the purpose of testing it. The bridge was made by the Hennebique Ferro-Concrete Construction Company (of France). It was noted: The bridge at Tuckton - replaces the wood and iron bridge of the Tuckton Bridge Co. which sold its undertaking to the Bournemouth Corporation for £15,000. It was constructed of concrete and iron throughout. It had a light and airy appearance with which it combined great strength and durability. It was 350' long, 29'6" wide and carried a double line of tramway plus a 6' footway on both sides. The largest span arch was at the centre 41' and there were 50 ferro-concrere piles. The Formal Opening was Tuesday 17th October 1905 although on picture evidence, it took much of this year to finish the works and finally dismantle the old wooden walkways of the original.
November 1908	Tramway receipts in the Borough are £90,500 with the Tuckton Bridge producing £1,837-10-0d. cf. to say £300 p.a. in 1888.
May 1909	Interest begins to grow in Hennebique and its revolutionary 'new' Ferro-concrete bridges.
October 1909	Early pleas are made to remove the tolls on Tuckton Bridge.
1921-1943	There follows over 20 years of continuous pressure to free the bridge of tolls (even though some fear an invasion of Southbourne by Christchurch tramps!) The trolleys when introduced bring no toll removal which has to wait to 1.10.1943 - the return by then ten fold original costs.

THE TRAMWAY EXTENSION TO CHRIST CHURCH: the Tram Procession
crossing Tuckton Bridge.

Water Colour Sketches of the District.

THE STUDIO
TUCKTON
CHRISTCHURCH

Mr W.G. HOOPER
requests the
honour of
a visit to view
his works

Exhibitor at the Royal Academy.

TELEPHONE No. 0196, CHRISTCHURCH,

Tuckton is an ancient settlement, far older than the early 20thC shopping parades we see today. The name derives from the Anglo-Saxon Toucketon or Touketon. With a ford near the present bridge, it provided a crossing of the Stour and so a secondary route to Christchurch though Wick Ferry and Ford seems to have held precedence. Forgotten largely however, it was perhaps best known as a Smugglers Haven by the 18thC, most other later activity revolving around the farm. Modern records trace the following events:

1841 Census Tuckton

Robert Brinson	40	Farmer
Mary Brinson	35	
Robert Brinson	7	
Emily Brinson	5	
Joanna Brinson	3	
Alfred Brinson	1	
Thomas Williams	30	Ag. lab.
Sarah Williams	30	
Mary Williams	3	
Eliza Williams	7 mos	
Richard Dale	45	Farmer
Sarah Dale	40	
Richard Dale	15	
Mary Dale	15	
Francis Dale	14	
Samuel Dale	12	
John Dale	19	
Marianne Pain	15	servant
John Holt	35	Ag. lab.
Priscilla Holt	35	
Elizabeth Holt	13	
Susan Holt	7	
Richard Street	45	Coast Guard
Susan Street	45	
John Randall	40	Ag. lab.
Martha Randall	40	
Robert Randall	20	Ag. lab.
Henry Randall	15	Ag. lab.
Marianne Randall	14	
Richard Randall	10	
Thomas Freeman	60	Ag. lab.
Jane Freeman	65	
Betsy Barnes	40	Independent
John Barnes	15	Ag. lab.
Louisa Barnes	4	
William King	75	Independent
Edward Troke	25	Ag. lab.
Henry Dale	45	Ag. lab.
Thomas Scott	40	Ag. lab.
Martha Scott	35	

Alfred Oliver	4	
William Oliver	2	
Mathilda Oliver	2 mos	
Mary Dunk	50	Nurse
George Ware	25	Ag. lab.
Ann Ware	25	
George Ware	6	
Edmund Ware	3	
Mathew Hale	35	
Eliza Hale	35	
Marianne Hale	15	
William Hale	15	Bricklayer's lab.
Maria Hale	11	
Henry Hale	9	
John Hale	4	
Sarah Hale	2	
Cecelia McMean	35	Independent
Sarah McMean	15	
Samuel McMean	12	
Mary McMean	11	
James Miller	35	Ag. lab.
James Miller	35	Ag. lab.
Hannah Miller	35	
Anna Miller	12	
Emma Miller	10	
Louisa Miller	6	
Eli Miller	3	
Andrew Miller	3	
Joseph Brinson	45	Ag. lab.
Susan Miller	40	
Sarah Miller	20	
Elizabeth Miller	15	
Mary Miller	7	
Henry Brinson	80	Ag. lab.
William Scott	12	
George Scott	10	
-	1 week	

1841 Census Hengistbury Tything of Tuckton

Name	Age	Occupation
John Marshall	55	Ag. lab.
Catherine Marshall	55	
John Marshall	25	Ag. lab.
William Marshall	20	Ag. lab.
Elizabeth Marshall	10	
Thomas Marshall	6	
Ellwood Day	35	Shipwright
Elizabeth Day	35	
James Day	8	
Margaret Day	4	
Christopher Day	2	
John Day	8 mos	
James Futcher	20	Coast Guard
James Wingate	45	do
Mary Hayward	40	Nurse
James Oliver	35	Mounted Guard
Mary Oliver	30	
Emily Oliver	6	

Census 1851 Tuckton Tything of Tuckton

Name	Age	Occupation
John Barnes	25	Ag. lab.
Elizabeth Barnes	25	
John Barnes	6	scholar
William Barnes	2	
George Barnes	8 mos	
James Collins	20	lodger Groom
Richard Dale	56	Farmer of 360 acres. employs 15 men.
Sarah Dale	52	
Samuel Dale	22	works on farm
Sarah Dale	18	
Ellen Dale	16	
Eliza Dale	14	scholar
Robert Dale	8	
Mary Curtis	18	House servant
Thomas Scott	42	Ag. lab.
Martha Scott	44	
William Scott	23	Ag. lab.
Charles Scott	9	scholar
Henry Scott	7	do
Edward Troke	34	lodger Carter
Henry Dale	60	lodger Ag. lab.
George Lilly	28	Ag. lab.
Elizabeth Lilly	25	cripple
Thomas Brenton	75	lodger Ag. lab.
William Summers	27	Ag. lab. Takes care of house.
James Summers	27	Ag. lab.
Timothy Collins	61	widower Coastguard Boatman.
Mary Collins	19	Dressmaker
Johanne Collins	17	Dressmaker
Timothy Kelley	1	grandson
Samuel Norris	60	Chief Boatman Coastguard
Elizabeth Norris	41	
Mary Norris	11	scholar
Amanda Norris	8	do
William McQuire	50	Boatman Coastguard
Eliza McQuire	50	
William McQuire	7	scholar
John Summers	69	Ag. lab.
Elizabeth Summers	69	
George Summers	3	grandson. Scholar at home.
John Summers	43	Ag. lab.
Jane Summers	37	
Ann Summers	15	Watch chain maker
George Summers	13	Ag. lab.
Eliza Summers	10	scholar

Mary Summers	4	scholar
Elizabeth Summers	8	do
Ellen Summers	2	
Metura Wheeler	80	widow Pauper

Wick House

John Sloman	45	Farmer of 113 acres. employs 5 labourers.
Louisa Sloman	42	
John Sloman	20	
Louisa Sloman	18	
Sarah Russell	20	servant
Harriett Atfield	21	do
Elizabeth Brackson	25	do
Robert Brinson	51	Dairyman
Mary Brinson	47	
Anne Brinson	20	Dairymaid
Robert Brinson	18	Ag. lab.
Emily Brinson	16	Dairymaid
Johanna Brinson	13	Dressmaker
Alfred brinson	11	scholar
William Veal	45	Master Mariner
Caroline Veal	41	
Harriett Veal	10	
Stephen Carlton	25	Farmer of 147 acres arable and 30 acres common Employs 5 labs.
Susan Carlton	23	
Stephen Carlton	11 mos	
Ann Hensight	17	House servant
George Parsons	52	Ag. lab.
Sarah Parsons	55	
Jane Parsons	23	Dressmaker
Leah Parsons	22	Watch chain maker
Eliza Parsons	18	do
John Pain	62	Ag. lab.
Ann Pain	60	Schoolmistress
Eliza Pain	29	Watch Chain Maker
Maria Pain	24	do
Ann Pain	2	grandchild
Ellen Pain	1	do
Ann Pain	92	Pauper
Hanna Pain	57	do
Thomas Brien	30	Ag. lab.
Fanny Brien	29	

Eliza Brien	10	scholar
Fanny Brien	8	do
John Brien	4	do
Rosa Pain	2	
James Miller	49	Ferryman
Annabella Miller	22	daughter Dressmaker
Emma Miller	19	Seamstress
Eli Miller	12	scholar
Eliza Miller	6	do
Levi Groves	31	Farmer 458 acres Employs 10 labs.
Maryanne Groves	30	
Levi Groves	10	scholar
Lucy Groves	8	do
Leonard Groves	6	do
Stephen Groves	3	do
John Groves	3 weeks	
Henry Gibbs	40	late Linen Draper
Hanna Miller	47	Nurse
Mary Brinsly	18	servant
Samuel Martin	35	Ag. lab.
Maryanne Martin	35	
Joshua Martin	9	scholar
Ann Martin	3	do
Ann Day		widow
Robert Bishop	49	Ag. lab.
Rebecca Bishop	50	
John Bishop	17	App shoemaker
Mary Bishop	17	Watch chain maker
Ann Bishop	15	do
George Bishop	13	Ag. lab
Elizabeth Bishop	11	Watch chain maker
Ellen Bishop	8	scholar
William Bishop	3	scholar at home
James Parsons	47	Ag. lab.
William Selwood	22	Ag. lab.
George Dean		Dairyman
Elizabeth Dean	20	
Charles Dean	1 month	
William Bendle	57	Ag. lab.
Harriett Bendle	64	
Elizabeth Brindle	21	Watch chain maker
Catherine Marshall	62	widow Pauper
Jane Marshall	24	Watch chain maker

Thomas Marshall   16   Ag. lab.
Timothy Starks   42   Ag. lab.
Louisa Starks   28
William Starks   3
Eliza Starks   1 month
Eliza Fry   17   Watch chain
                       maker
John Frampton   30   Gardener
Caroline Frampton 31
Edward Frampton 8
Charles Frampton 5
John Frampton   8 months
Charlotte Shambler 66 Nurse

Warren

John Marshall   34   Ag. lab.
Sarah Marshall   30
Ellen Marshall   3
John Marshall   1
William Troke   24   Brickmaker

1851 Census Hengistbury

Hengistbury Head Watch House
William Morris   32   Boatman
                       Coastguard
Thomas Jones   34   do
George Wickham   60   Carter
Jane Wickham   56
James Read   42   Brickmaker
Mary Read   38
James Read   17   Invalid
Abraham Read   14   Labourer
Isaac Read   9   scholar
George Read   5   scholar at home
Albert Read   2
John Read   17   lodger labourer
Edward Lawrence   27   Labourer
Maryanne Lawrence 25
Eliza Lawrence   1
George Hinton   28   Labourer
Esther   39
Elizabeth Hinton 10   scholar at home
Edward Pearce   30   Labourer
Sarah Pearce   26
Elizabeth Pearce 3   scholar at home
William Bishop   23   Labourer
George Ivemy   13   Under carter

The Lively Cutter hauled up and fitted as a residence for:

Richard Aswell   35   Commission
                       Coastguard
                       Boatman
Sarah Aswell   34
Sarah Aswell   3
William Aswell   5
Edward Aldridge   33   Boatman
                       Coastguard
Martha Aldridge   30
Henry Messenger   30   Boatman
                       Coastguard
Lucy Messenger   29

April 1860	An alteration takes place to the local coastguard when Bournemouth Station becomes 3 (Tuckton, Bournemouth and Flaghead). These cover the bay from Warren to N.Haven.
March 1862	Charles Love, one of the preventive men stationed at Tuckton has a narrow escape in a gun accident.
July 1864	There is a Tuckton's Mill at Hern (sic) said to be "beautiful but weedy" like much of the local Stour.
April 1865	A court case takes place re (Richard) Dale's land at Tuckton.
Summer 1871	Dale (according to Mate & Riddle) details his reservations about the now burgeoning growth of Bournemouth consequent upon the national freeing up of capital. He feared that, already, the "greatest beauties" of the area south of the Stour had been "robbed". As he saw, "When I look back to the beginning of this century, when...many thousand acres were clothed with beautiful heather, millions of busy bees collecting from its lovely flowers, when I reflect on the past and think of the present I can hardly feel that the world is progressing, but retrograding in these days. The bee garden was by the side of the common from Wick to Wimborne, on to Corfe and to Lytchett. The hives were placed and they swarmed and stayed until September...And from what I have been told the district was much healthier" before the fir plantations grew and the beautiful plateau lost its covering of numerous flower varieties.
October 1874	One of the Tuckton coastguardmen finds a body washed up on the Western Shore (14th).
November 1880	'Alarmists' fear the loss of the ferry at Wick when the first Tuckton Bridge (wooden version) is completed. However they discover the ferry in question is an extinct route at the bottom of Green Low Lane "just where the bridge is to be." "No one has used the ferry for years and no one wants to."
February 1881	The proposed new bridge over the Stour (Engineer Crouch) becomes the biggest issue to excite the local community for many years. Should it be toll or free?
Summer 1882	The Waterworks in Iford Lane in process of construction.
November 1884	The new Wimborne & Christchurch (S&D?) Railway is outlined to run via Iford, Tuckton and Wick to a port to be made in the Harbour. In Tuckton it was seen it would pass right through the local rookery. Meantime Iford Bridge was widened as local traffic increased.
May 1886	The opening takes place of the new Christchurch Station connected now to Tuckton & Southbourne by the new Stour Road (30th).

June 1886	There is a shoeing Smith's shop at Tuckton run by Charles Luffman.

September 1887   The quarterly practice of the coastguard takes place at the Tuckton Station (19th). 12 men, under Divisional Officer, Herbert (of Swanage) took part in life saving exercises.

August 1888   Southbourne Pier opened on the 6th. Many more people now pass through the district than hitherto and especially following the completion of the new Bournemouth railway improvements.

March 1890   The poor state of the footpaths over Tuckton Bridge is complained of. There are fears these may help rot the wooden bridge. In addition, the road between Tuckton & Wick is reported in a dangerous condition.

May 1891   Tuckton House is sold.

November 1892   Laura Kate Tuersley is drowned near Tuckton Bridge.

Summer 1894   Tolstoy is said to have enjoyed a Tuckton holiday this year.

November 1897   Boating is now available at Tuckton.

December 1898   Tuckton Bridge toll house is reported to be in a "wretched condition".

March 1899   W.G. Hooper (of Wick) has established his artists studio in Tuckton. The Tuckton Mission Hall is also in existence.

Gun Competition at Tuckton

The annual prize competition on the 64 pounder R.M.L. of the 1st and 2nd batteries (Bournemouth) of the 2nd Volunteer (Dorset) Brigade S.D.R.A. took place on Saturday afternoon at Tuckton. The weather during the afternoon was very unfavourable, a drizzling rain falling nearly all the time. The officers present were Major Rebbeck, Adjutant and Capt. Clarke (who acted as umpire) and Surgeon Denman (as time keeper) - There were 5 detactments competing with the following as No. 1's - No.1 detachment Sgt. Lacey; No. 2 detachment Sgt. Habgood; No. 3 detachment Sgt. Collins; No. 4 detachment Sgt. Major Hawker and No. 5 detachment Sgt. Major Riggs. Four trial shots were fired and then the competition commenced. Sgt. Lacey's detachment firing first, the others following in rotation. Some very good practice was made and in good time. The range was 1712 yards, each detachment firing 3 shots. The result of the competition is not known yet, but will be given later in the week.

Bournemouth Observer, 3.10.1888

Summer 1900   Stourfield Estate begins its development.

October 1901   The Tuckton Russian Colony is established (see below).

March 1902	The local artist, Mr. W.G. Hooper, of Tuckton, near Christchurch has some pictures ready for sending to the Royal Academy. One large painting, entitled 'Lingering Daylight' an evening effect, with cows dimly seen in a meadow, also a water colour view of the River Stour at Christchurch; and other smaller works. The pictures are on view at the studio, Tuckton from Monday 17th 'til Saturday the 22nd inst. between 3 and 5 o'clock each day and Mr. Hooper was "pleased to show them to any persons interested, on presentation of address card."
November 1903	Death of Captain Lamb, Tuckton. A Mr. Waham "a well known taxidermist of Carisbrooke, Isle of Wight" places 1080 Rudd in the Stour (c.25th).
May 1904	A fire breaks out on George Carter's farm at Tuckton - the work of arsonist John Barrow who was later apprehended in Boscombe. The other farms were Elfords and Stourcliff, run by George Kellaway.
September 1904	Vladimer Tchertkoff (sic) gives a talk about Tolstoy - in Tuckton.
October 1904	Another Tuckton lecture. There are many cultural events in this still tiny hamlet.
January 1905	The Council is now in possession of Tuckton Bridge - a theme of local correspondence throughout this year.
February 1905	The Russian Colony remain local celebrities.
August 1905	Poachers are known to be active off Tuckton lane.
September 1905	The new Tuckton Bridge proceeds towards completion as do the tramway company's lines to Christchurch via Southbourne.
October 1905	Opening of the Poole-Christchurch tramway viz Tuesday 17.10.1905. The Hennebique Ferro Concrete Construction Company's bridge has replaced the older wooden and iron one which the TB Co. sold to Bournemouth Corporation for £15,000.
April 1908	The pulling down of another old thatched roofed cottage at Pokesdown points to the coming end of this form of picturesque dwelling in Bournemouth. There were not many left now and they were thought "all doomed except perhaps an odd few in the almost unknown area of Wick & Tuckton, where, probably, civilization will be the longest in stretching out its claws." Everywhere, "the useful and efficient is ousting the merely ornamental." (cf. Studland).
May 1908	Mrs. Phoebe Nutter Scott gives evidence at the Emma Sherriff murder trial. She is the wife of the proprietor of Tuckton Creeks and lives at Tuckton Lawn. The body was found near the gate and Rocket Post on the Western Shore.

August 1908	Vladimir Tchertkoff - the founder of the 50 strong Tuckton Russian colony from 1901, and its associated <u>Free Age Press</u> for the publication of the works of Tolstoy, was exiled from Russia in 1898. This took place because of "his active support of the Doukhobors - a persecuted people now settled in Canada." A photograph of him with Tolstoy may be seen in the <u>National Geographic Magazine</u>, June 1986, p. 771. Apparently, the Tuckton colony lived in "comfortable poverty" - Army camp beds and deal furniture, few blinds or curtains. Tchertkoff (Kov) became Tolstoy's sole literary executor and died age 82 in 1937 long after his return to Russia in 1908 where interestingly, he upset the Governor of Tula and was part exiled again. His mother was a member of the Royal Court.
September 1908	There is a tramway accident at Tuckton. Meanwhile Count Chertkov (Tchertkoff) is allowed to return to Russia. (He died there in 1937).
May 1909	William Nutter Scott (of the Tuckton Creeks) is a witness in a local burglary case.
October 1909	The first of many pleas are heard to remove the tolls on Tuckton Bridge.
July 1910	Bournemouth Centenary Air Show takes place on land astride today's Broadway - the canvas hangars being sited in front of the newly built, 1908, Broom Close house.
January 1911	William N. Scott "the last of the old residents of Tuckton" has died.
February 1911	Tuckton Mission Hall continues its meetings. The Hetherlea property (occupied by E.W. Douglas) in the village - sold, meanwhile.
March 1911	Death of Hon. Douglas at Tuckton and funeral. A memorial park is suggested. Meantime, the French Gardens, near Tuckton Bridge (Stour Road) are open and charge a 6d entrance fee.
November 1911	Mudeford v Old Tucktonians. The place is big enough for football teams.
June 1912	Tuckton boating and singing. A fete is held at Tuckton Creeks on the 8th, ladies and gentlemen "contributing vocal and instrumental items."
November 1913	The Daily Mail airman Henri Salmet, announces his intention to visit Bournemouth (on 29th) and give flying exhibitions in a 80 h.p. Bleriot machine. He is to use a large enclosed field at Tuckton Farm belonging to A. Bartlett. He crashes.
September 1916	The Will of R.H. Carter of Wick (who died at Jutland 21.5.1916) is read. He was the eldest son of the late Rear Admiral Richard Carter of

Wick. Despite the war - riverside 'travelogues' appear in the local press.

| August 1920 | Christchurch Regatta's first revival after the War. |

| May 1921 | Teas are now available at the Old Water Works (Kiddles), once the Russian's printing works in Iford Lane. |

| June 1921 | The Tuckton Creeks advertises itself - so indicating the increasing riverside trade of these years. |

| July/August 1921 | A young man of 18 is drowned in a canoe accident near Tuckton (Wednesday 20th) whilst the following month a punter is drowned 150 yards from the Riverside Terrace boathouse. John Charles Edmonds, boat proprietor of Wick Ferry and the hirer of the punt gave evidence. |

| March 1923 | Newlyn & Ball take over the Tuckton Creeks site. They make a new balcony and tealounge. |

| June 1923 | First local sign of the postwar housebuilding movement is the sale of the Iford estate. Soon another tiny riverside community will lose its character forever. |

| August 1923 | 218 Hampshire Battery mounted sports day held by Tuckton Bridge. |

| August 1924 | More sales of land take place around Wick. |

| July 1925 | Riverland Estate & Brightlands are offered for sale - the first moves towards the lonely Headland. |

| April 1926 | The Southern Railway plans to make a new goods yard and station on land near Iford viz near Stourfield Council school and on part of its playground. Bournemouth councillors oppose the scheme at access roads are poor and the site is too far from the town centre. Homefield School opens this year. |

| June 1926 | The sale of Tuckton Farm. Following its announcement in January, the £7,500 Iford lane widening scheme gets approval. It serves the toll free bridge at Iford and runs attractively alongside the river for part of its length - which part the Corporation plan to make into a riverside walk. There is also to be a 'pleasure garden' just south of the railway set on what at that time were river meadows near the old Waterworks. Madam & Mrs. V. Tcherkoff (sic) were giving a strip of their Tuckton House lands to help the road improvement. The general idea was a far sighted attempt (lead by Dolamore - the Borough Engineer) to provide expanding Bournemouth with the elements of a green belt. |

| August 1931 | The opening of the Athelstan Pub (near Tuckton). |

| October 1931 | A building estate is announced for Iford Lane just as the new Iford bridge is under construction. |

| February 1933 | Opening of Iford bridge. First Trolleys in prospect. |

| April 1933 | Concern is expressed for "lovely Wick Lane" under pressure from "the increasing population of Tuckton." The Trolleys arrive this May. Now, until 1939, more and more building, in tandem with the national expansion, will appear in all the suburbs of Bournemouth. |

| Mid 1930's | Considerable building work continues, infilling plots in Carbery and associated avenues. The many empty sites around the Water Tower begin to disappear as the building boom expands. |

| November 1935 | More floods reach record levels at Iford Bridge where divers and steam shovels had been widening and deepening the river for some months. The golf course at Tuckton Bridge was swamped, once again, for it was in reality, the river's flood plain. |

1939-45

Following the Second World War, Tuckton had just a few years of relative quiet while national recovery went ahead, and then rapid development began once more - the remaining green fields giving way to bungalows and the old Belle Vue Road Junction at Tuckton to a new roundabout. Many trees were lost as were the last meadows behind today's Riverside Inn - long the scene of fetes, events and November firework celebrations. In 1948, the Peek Toy Trading Co. established itself in a remaining part of Tuckton Farm - while the Machine shop of Lander & Co was originally the main barn of the Manor. In Iford Lane, Homefield School under S.C. Taggart developed its career while, in 1951, the Tuckton Traders Association was founded - soon active in the matter of further proposed developments along the Broadway where rival shops &c were planned. Everywhere the rural 'feel' of the district was giving way to a suburbanised one - open fields being banished to well beyond Broom Close by 1960.

| March 1954 | 200 people pack the Tuckton Tea Gardens to hear Bournemouth Councillors outline proposed Hengistbury Head developments. The Tuckton New Church Society holds meetings. |

| April 1954 | Tuckton Traders are against the Broadway shops planned, plus associated petrol station. |

| May 1954 | There are new plans announced for Broom Close. |

| July 1954 | A family of 3 are saved after a rowing boat accident near Tuckton Bridge. |

| September 1954 | There is a new scheme announced for a riverside walk besides the Stour - part of the Bournemouth development plan for this area. |

| March 1955 | Sale of Solent Meads Estate, part one. |

September 1955	The Tuckton Traders Association - Membership 53 - continues to operate even though it almost 'packed up in crisis' 21 months ago.
March 1956	The New Broadway Shops are soon to open which does not overmuch please those in Tuckton.
May 1956	It is announced that the Houseboats (MTB's mainly) are "to go".
March 1958	There is opposition to the Bridge House Hotel and Riverside Club obtaining a licence as a public house (today's Riverside Inn). New bungalows nearby have only just been completed.
April 1958	Tuckton wrecks riddle. Three sunken boats in the Stour near Tuckton Bridge are about to be dragged out. (Avon & Dorset River Board.)
May 1958	Solent Meads Estate (No. 2 sale).
June 1958	The filling in of the horseshoe reedy creek near Tuckton Tea Gardens gets underway. It is hoped to complete this by the end of the year and elsewhere, down to Wick Ferry, by 1961.
May 1959	The barge 'Merle' - sunk near Tuckton Bridge 20 months ago, and still in the river, is deemed a "total loss". (The barge was launched but sunk in June 1957.)
December 1959	The Stour now flows past the horseshoe creek at Tuckton - so marking the end of this once teeming reed bed.
January 1960	Memories of the Russian Colony and their "secret press" are rekindled.
February 1963	Tuckton now gets attention from the local newspapers as it has grown strongly to be deemed "a shopping centre in its own right".
August 1965	Mrs. Gladys Adams and family (3 daughters) operate the Tuckton Tea Gardens.
September 1965	Regatta (4th) has £200 of fireworks. The long tradition continues.
April 1969	Trolley buses come to an end in the week of the 18th.
1971 to date	For the modern period at Tuckton, readers may wish to refer to the local published sources - notably the several editions of The Last Village on the Dorset Stour and J.A. Young's Tuckton today and Yesterday. In general, much has continued here as might be expected, the last infilling of the east side of the shopping centre coming in the 1970's and then the part rebuilding of Tuckton Bridge as the prodigious traffic flows across it took an increasing and other kind of toll. Today it would be interesting to compare vehicle numbers with those very few

recorded in the 1887 return, probably something of the order of 12,500 cars &c crossing per day compared to the 250, of all kinds, then.

Otherwise flooding and flood protection works (drains and walls) have been strong features of the 1980's and latterly, of course, the problem of the restoration of Wick Ferry (set for early Summer 1993) - for so many, a near vital short cut and service. The 'watch on the Stour' in brief, has further yet to run.

Christchurch.   Wick Ferry

THE CENTENARY AIR PAGEANT

In 1910, Bournemouth set out to show "that an aviation meeting (could) be held in England in the continental way". The organizers chose a fine site, the <u>Morning Leader</u> stating "the ground (was) more picturesquely situated than any at which such a gathering has been held in this country"... the "very setting of the flights will add to their sensationalism."

The meeting was set to open on Monday 11th July and to continue for 6 days of flying. Additionally, and as part of the Bournemouth Centenary celebrations, there were to be carnivals, a motorcar gymkhana, flower battles, fetes and athletic meetings plus evening concerts, parades and a fancy dress ball.

To secure the site at Southbourne, a large fence was put up to exclude "gatecrashers". "Great care has been taken to screen the aerodrome from the view of non paying persons by means of close boarded fencing and canvas screens. Something like 6 miles of timber and canvas, ranging from 4'6" to 16' in height, have been used for the purpose."

The layout of the course may be seen from the attached diagram but to further help with its location it may be noted that the hangars lay alongside Wick Lane just west of today's Broom Close Library. The long lane E.W. extending from them was Broadway Lane, today's Thornbury Road - the most easterly pylon being approximately on the later Broadway site of the (now demolished) Saxon King Hotel. At this time the ground was mainly ploughed fields criss-crossed by recently grubbed out ancient hedgerows.

BOURNEMOUTH CENTENARY AVIATION MEETING.
MR C. GRAHAME-WHITE.

LIST OF COMPETITORS: INTERNATIONAL AVIATION MEETING

Four pylons were used to set out the 3,140 yard course: (Monday July 11-16th, 6 days). The 19 pilots were:-

Edmond AUDEMARS (Swiss)	DEMOISELLE monoplane
G.A. BARNES	HUMBER
Alan BOYLE	AVIS monoplane
CHRISTIAENS (Belgian)	FARMAN biplane
Col. Samuel Franklin CODY (U.S.A.)	CODY
COLMORE	SHORT
J. Armstrong DREXEL (U.S.A.)	BLERIOT
Capt. Bertram DICKSON	FARMAN
L.D.L. GIBBS	SOMMER FARMAN
Cecil GRACE	SHORT
Claude GRAHAME-WHITE	FARMAN & BLERIOT

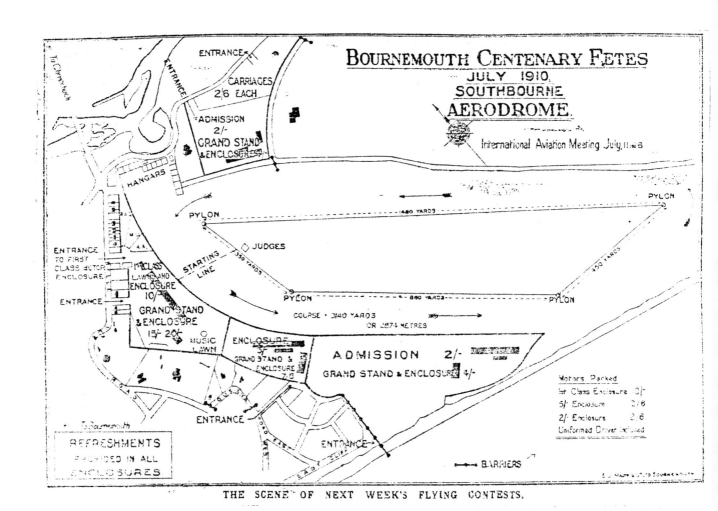

THE SCENE OF NEXT WEEK'S FLYING CONTESTS.

Robert 'Jones' LORAINE	FARMAN
J.T.C. MOORE BRABAZON	SHORT & VOISIN
Leon MORANE (France)	BLERIOT
Alex OGILVIE	SHORT-WRIGHT
J. RADLEY	BLERIOT
Major Alfred RAWLINSON	FARMAN
Charles Stewart ROLLS	FARMAN & WRIGHT
WAGNER	HANRIOT

Note: 15 British pilots (inc. McArdle) were amongst the flyers and 10 British built machines were used in the contest. The meeting was the "first (of its type) in the British Isles." William Edward McArdle (Mortormac) was Bournemouth's first pilot whilst Moore Brabazon was the first man to get a pilot's licence in England. (For full details and the effects of Rolls' death, see The Brabazon Story, 1956. The licence is dated 8.3.1910.

Only the year before (1909) Louis Bleriot had completed the first Channel flight whilst, in 1910 Rolls (the first Briton to die in powered flight) did it both ways.

PRIZE LIST

Longest Flight	-	£3,000 first, £150 second, £60 third, £30 fourth.
Speed Flight	-	£1,000 first prize, £400 second, other prizes £100 and £50.
Greatest Altitude	-	Prizes same as in speed flight.
Getting off & Alighting	-	Prizes from £250 to £25 for the first four.
Sea Flight	-	£800 first prize, £400 second, £100 third.
Weight carrying	-	£350 first prize, £150 second, £50 third.
General Merit	-	£500 first prize, £300 second, £150 third, £50 fourth.
Slowest Circuit	-	One prize £100.
Competitions for Assistants	-	Two prizes £60 and £40 [£8,500 aggregate].
Daily Telegraph Prize	-	Silver Cup for the British Aviator "giving the best exhibition on any machine."

Winners: Leon Morane (France) £3,425; Grahame White (U.K.) £1,350; and J. Armstrong Drexel (U.S.A.) £1,125.

THE SITE

"It is difficult to realise that a few months ago the stretch of meadows slightly undulating to the sea, with all the glories of the Solent in full view, and the exquisite landscape crowned by Christchurch Priory presenting an opposite picture , was a hedge crossed, sloping vista of English countryside, studded with cabbage patches, sheep enclosures and odd farm buildings. It was only after anxious survey that the site of the Aerodrome was suggested, and fortunately for the Committee every facility was willingly afforded for its temporary acquirement by the owners of the ground."

"The first work of the Centenary Committee was to clear, drain and level the ground (? involving the final demolition of Cellars Farm). Nearly three miles of hedges and earth banks had to be removed and something like forty small vegetable allotments expunged and their owners reasonably compensated. The work and serious expense involved can be imagined.

THE CENTENARY CELEBRATIONS AT BOURNEMOUTH
A GUIDE TO THE VARIOUS FÊTES

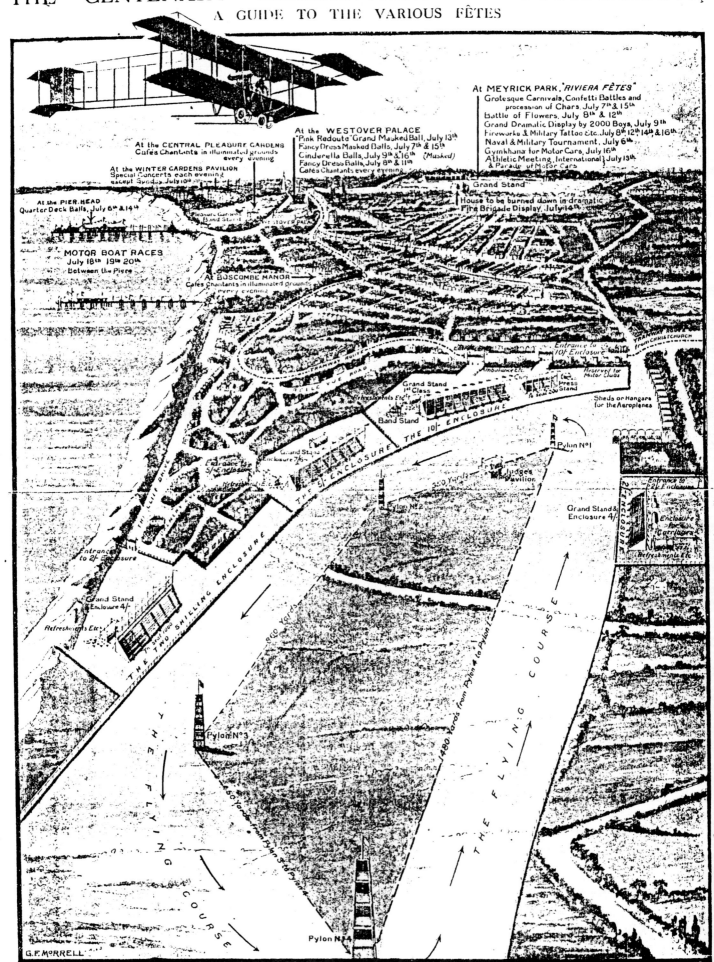

At the CENTRAL PLEASURE GARDENS
Cafés Chantants in illuminated grounds every evening

At the WINTER GARDENS PAVILION
Special Concerts each evening except Sunday, July 10th

At the PIER HEAD
Quarter Deck Balls, July 6th & 14th

MOTOR BOAT RACES
July 18th 19th 20th Between the Piers

At BOSCOMBE MANOR
Cafés Chantants in illuminated grounds every evening

At the WESTOVER PALACE
"Pink Redoute" Grand Masked Ball, July 13th
Fancy Dress Masked Balls, July 7th & 15th
Cinderella Balls, July 9th & 16th (Masked)
Fancy Dress Balls, July 8th & 11th
Cafés Chantants every evening

At MEYRICK PARK, "RIVIERA FÊTES"
Grotesque Carnivals, Confetti Battles and procession of Chars, July 7th & 15th
Battle of Flowers, July 8th & 12th
Grand Dramatic Display by 2000 Boys, July 9th
Fireworks & Military Tattoo etc. July 8th 12th 14th & 16th
Naval & Military Tournament, July 6th
Gymkhana for Motor Cars, July 16th
Athletic Meeting, International July 13th
& Parade of Motor Cars

Grand Stand
House to be burned down in dramatic Fire Brigade Display, July 14th

TRAM to CHRISTCHURCH

Entrance to 10/ Enclosure
Ambulance Etc.
Reserved for Motor Clubs
Press Stand
Sheds or Hangars for the Aeroplanes

Grand Stand 1st Class
Refreshments Etc
Band Stand

THE 10/ ENCLOSURE

Pylon No 1

Entrance to 2/ Enclosure
Enclosure for Corporations
Refreshments Etc.

Grand Stand & Enclosure 4/

Judges Pavilion

Pylon No 2

Grand Stand Enclosure 7/6
Refreshments E.C.
Entrance 5/ enclosure

THE 5/ ENCLOSURE
THE HALF DRIVE

Entrance to 2/ Enclosure

Grand Stand Enclosure 4/
Refreshments Etc.

THE TWO SHILLING ENCLOSURE

THE FLYING COURSE

Pylon No 3

1480 Yards from Pylon 4 to Pylon 1

THE FLYING COURSE

Pylon No 4

G.F. MORRELL

Bournemouth is now in the midst of the series of brilliant fêtes whereby the town is commemorating its centenary, but the most attractive feature of the celebrations—the international Aviation Meeting—does not begin till next Monday. The aerodrome, or aviation ground, is magnificently situated overlooking the Solent and within easy reach of the town. Fifteen British airmen and four foreign champions are competing, the principal prizes—of a total value of £5500—being given for the longest flight, the speed flight, the greatest altitude, and the best flight over the

DRAWN BY G. F. MORRELL

However, the Aerodrome, as it is now presented, shows to a certain extent a natural basin, but very level and extending about two miles from the main road to the sea coast. There is, perhaps, only a deviation of two feet to the level, but the general height above sea and entire freedom from any obstructing trees or buildings will give the most perfect view of the aviation from every corner of the Aerodrome. From the first pylon at the S.E. corner of the course to the second pylon on the S.W. side is a distance of 350 yards. From pylon No. 2 to pylong No. 3 there is a flight of 860 yards. Then to pylon 4 seawards, is a further 450 yards, with a turn flight home of some 1,400 yards, or nearly a mile, the total distance of the flying course being just under two miles."

Grandstand   Seating for 1500 people plus a band, velvety lawns, refreshment rooms and first class restaurant, telephone and P.O., ambulance and police huts.

Second Class
Grandstand   Seating for 1000 people with similar facilities.

Third Class stands   Seating for 2,000, 1,000 each.
                                              Also press stand for 200 newsmen.

Also ample car parks, standing of carriages, stalling of horses, stacking of bicycles etc. "at very nominal charges".

Christchurch Head, a natural landmark rising above the sea cliff and forming a natural point of vantage, has been secured for the purpose of giving spectators a view of sea flights round the Isle of Wight and, for a nominal fee transfers (were) issued from the various enclosures to the headland.

There was also a 2 minute service of trams making the 20 minute run from the Square. Christchurch Station had special trains.
                                              Morning Leader, 11.7.1910

DAYS OF AIR PAGEANT

Noon. Sunday 10th July. Dramatic unofficial opening by W.E. McArdle in a Bleriot monoplane.

Mon. 11th July 1910   "Competitions for the longest flight, speed, altitude, starting, alighting, oversea flight (to the Needles and back) weight carrying, general merit and slow flying." The prizes totalled £8,500.

Tuesday 12th July   C.S. Rolls is killed when attempting an alighting competition on a fixed spot. "The flying was at once suspended and the large gathering dispersed."

Wed. 13th July   The meeting was resumed in the morning but the weight carrying competition was removed from the programme as "anything of the nature of trick flying" was now not permitted. 10,000 people attended with several hundred cars "in the motor enclosure". Weather: gloriously fine.

Thurs. 14th July   "Nothing of great interest happened until late in the afternoon". A grey mist had descended and "almost turned day into night". Banks of grey cloud obscured Morane's altitude attempt. At 7 o'clock in the evening Major Alfred Rawlinson was injured in another accident.

Fri. 15th July   Windy conditions prevented flying until the afternoon sea flight to the Needles. Sea mist over the water.

Sat. 16th July   "Rain and wind (framed) a silent aerodrome." Some flying on a 'rain shrouded' course took place with some flying competitions completed by the end of the day.

THE TOLL OF THE AIR

After Rolls' fatal crash it was noted how, "Since the beginning of the present year (1910), seven airmen have lost their lives while engaged in flight with heavier than air machines. Three fatalities occurred last year, and 1 in 1908."

The death roll was as follows:

Lieutenant Selfridge at Washington	11.9.1908
M. Lefebvre at Juvisy	7.9.1909
Capt. Ferber at Boulogne	22.9.1909
Senor.Fernandez at Nice	6.12.1909
M. Delagrange at Bordeaux	4.1.1910
M. Le Blon at San Sebastian	2.4.1910
M. Michelin at Lyons	13.5.1910
M. Zosily at Budapest	2.6.1910
Herr Robl at Stettin	18.6.1910
M. Wachter at Rheims	3.7.1910
Mr. C.S. Rolls at Bournemouth	12.7.1910

Note: Bournemouth's pioneer aviator, William E. McArdle a pilot at Wallisdown's Flying Whit Week 1910 who later started the motor industry in Bournemouth, died in 1935.

Paper Sources

Morning Leader	11.7.1910
Daily Echo	20.7.1910
Bournemouth Guardian	5.7.1910
Daily Telegraph	6.7.1910
Bournemouth Directory	6.7.1910
Daily Chronicle	7.7.1910
Daily Telegraph	7th & 8th. 7.1910
The Globe	9.7.1910
Daily News	8.7.1910

Bournemouth Echo	8.7.1910
Morning Post	8.7.1910 and 11.7.1910
Bournemouth Guardian	9.7.1910
The Sketch	20.7.1910

AFTERMATH

March 1911

Bournemouth Centenary Fetes deficiency

They cost   £35,660
Receipts were £15,900
Deficit   £19,760

The International Aviation Meeting produced £7,286 and the expenditure was £18,461.

May 1912

Airman's Claim for damages v. Centenary Fete

This action arose out of an accident at the Bournemouth Meeting in July 1910 when the Hon. C.S. Rolls was killed.

The Plaintiff (Alfred Rawlinson) claimed compensation for a broken leg and £400 for his Farman aeroplane plus the return of his £40 entrance fees - all from the Committee of the Bournemouth Corporation which managed the meeting.

Apparently what happened "was that there was an old occupation road across the course which had been filled up with soft earth. All that was seen was that it was apparently level grass." The aviator claimed he had a right to expect that landing in the course would be reasonably safe. The road was 20 feet wide and had looked perfectly level.

Counsel added that having come down on the roadway the wheels of the aeroplane sank into the earth in spite of its skids or runners "and coming to a small bank opposite, pitched forward, putting an absolutely unbearable strain on the supports and bringing the mechanism heavily upon the ground." Rawlinson was thrown forward and injured. He underwent three operations.

Witnesses included W.E. McArdle who reported the course seems quite adequate to him, Major John Charles Kennedy of the Royal Engineers - a marshall of the course and the man looking after the hangars etc. and Charles Gray, a representative of the Aerodrome who declared "the course was a good average one for its purpose." E. Lander reported how he was first on the scene as the plane came down 'WOP'. Rawlinson at the time, declared the accident to be "all his fault".

The Jury found that the defendants had put the ground in proper form for an aviation meeting and that the plaintiff did not cross the filled in road.

THE HON. C. S. ROLLS' FATAL FLIGHT.

On Tuesday the Hon. C. S. Rolls met with a fatal accident. Mr. Rolls was flying in an "alighting" competition, and was approaching the alighting circle when the rear rudders, which had been added to the original design, broke loose from their framework, and the wires controlling them became entangled in the chains and propellers. The machine fell with great force from a height of about 40 feet, and was completely wrecked. Mr. Rolls died almost immediately.

THE INQUEST.

The inquest was held at the Borough Mortuary, Littledown road, at nine o'clock Wednesday morning. Two witnesses only were called, and the inquiry only lasted about twenty minutes. With the Borough Coroner (Mr. F. G. Lefroy) was the Mayor (Councillor G. E. Bridge). The foreman of the jury was Mr. W. E. Odlum.—The jury having been sworn and the body viewed, the Coroner, who was one of the stewards at the Aviation meeting, and witnessed the disaster, said he was sure the jury would agree with him that they should take the evidence very briefly—simply in regard to identity, the fall, and the doctor's evidence.—The jury generally assented.—The first witness was the Mr. V. Ker-Seymer, secretary of the meeting, of 119, Piccadilly, London. He said: On Tuesday, July 12th, I was at the Aerodrome, Southbourne, and saw deceased in the air on a Short-Wright biplane. This was about one o'clock. I saw the machine descend to the earth with great impact. I identify deceased as being the Hon. Charles Stewart Rolls, of South Lodge, Rutland Gate, London. His age was 33 years.—Dr. George Hammond Field, of Christchurch road, Boscombe, was the next witness. He said: I was on medical duty at the Aerodrome, and about 1 p.m. I saw deceased come to the ground with the machine. I at once went to him, and I believe when I first got there deceased was alive, but he died within a minute. The cause of death was concussion and laceration of the brain.—The Coroner: We all know that the medical staff and the ambulance corps did everything in their power to help.—The jury then returned a verdict in accordance with the medical evidence—through misadventure.

The following account of the accident was given by Mr. Roger Wallace, K.C., the president of the Aero Club:—"I was in the judge's box at the time of the catastrophe. I saw that Mr. Rolls was taking his dive at too high an altitude, and either the elevating plane broke in the air or else the chain or some of the stays gave way; I saw some fragments of material fall before the machine came to the earth. I have arranged with three clerks of the course, to examine the machine, with Mr. Grahame White, and give their opinion of the cause of the disaster. The real reason will not be known until these gentlemen have made their inspection. They will be Major Lindsey Lloyd (of the Brooklands Automobile Club), Mr. Dunville, and Mr. Bucknill."

Captain Maitland, in the course of a short conversation, said he saw the accident from a comparatively short distance. The first thing that called his attention to it was a loud snap before the machine had reached the ground. He distinctly saw something break away in the rudder, and this caused the machine to dive. He considered that the accident was caused entirely by the rudder giving way, owing to the immense strain put upon the machine in making a landing in the high wind. Before landing, in his opinion, the tail broke away, and the wires and tail crumpled up in the air. The machine was thus smashed to pieces on touching the ground.

Captain Dickson, who was also present, said that Mr. Rolls came down at too sharp an angle. The wind was too strong for him. In making a "vol plane" the head of a machine was turned down and the ignition was generally cut off. Then the machine came down like a shot from a pistol. Mr. Rolls had not cut off his engine, so that he must have come down all the faster. Capt. Dickson thinks that nothing was broken until the machine touched the ground. The accident, he says, was exactly similar to that which happened to Wachter at Rheims.

THE ACCIDENT.

The accident happened in front of the grand stand. Mr. Rolls went up with his French-built Wright biplane at 25 minutes past 12 o'clock in an attempt to win the alighting prize. This prize is awarded to the competitor who, after flying over a prescribed course, alights within a marked circle representing an island of 100 yards diameter, and brings his machine to a stop nearest to the centre. Mr. Grahame White had succeeded earlier in the morning in getting within 43ft. 3in. of the bull's-eye. Mr. Rolls in one attempt had stopped 78ft. 10in. from the centre, and in attempting to improve on this he met with the accident. He ascended and made one small circle, gradually increasing his altitude. Then, in a wider circle, he swept over the motor enclosure at great speed with a following wind, and he headed round at the back of the grand stand, coming into the teeth of the wind and riding down on a steep gradient towards the alighting point. Passing over the lawn at a height of 70ft., he stopped his motor and began to glide down at an angle of 40deg. in an effort to use the opposing wind so as to avoid a long run on the ground. To check the descent and to alight on the landing wheels of the machine, Mr. Rolls brought the elevating planes up very sharply. In this Wright machine, which is the same as that in which Mr. Rolls achieved the double crossing of the Channel, there is a tail plane, which is intended to secure some of the longtitudinal flight stability that is obtained with the Farman and other biplanes. This tail is a monoplane horizontal piece close to the two vertical rudder planes, and it moves in unison with the elevating planes in front, but of course in the opposite way. Thus, when the front planes are tilted upwards the tail plane has its leading-edge depressed. When he crossed the Channel Mr. Rolls had a similar tail plane, but it was fixed and he believed that it greatly assisted stability, but that it tended to counteract the effect of the movements of the elevator. Therefore he changed it for the new adjustable "stabilizer," which is a Wright patent. The new plane was attached last Sunday, and Mr. Rolls flew with it on Tuesday, when it certainly increased the facility with which upward and downward movements could be made. The sudden air pressure on the tail plane caused by the airman's apparently rather violent pull on the lever made it give way. The machine was at an altitude of about 50 feet when the left side of the tail plane broke away with part of the left of the rudder. In an instant there was a sound as of splitting wood, and the elevating plane swung back, the connecting gear no doubt, being all disarranged. The crowd saw what had happened and the horror of the sight compelled silence as the machine turned a complete somersault. In that position it fell straight to the ground from a height of from thirty to forty feet. The crash was followed by the explosion of the motor. The first arrivals at the spot found Mr. Rolls lying clear of the broken machine. So far as could be seen he had not been badly cut. He was lifted up and placed on one of the broken planes, and as there was some slight movement of the body an attempt was made at artificial respiration. On Dr. Hardy coming up ether was administered. The doctor, nevertheless, expressed the opinion that death had been instantaneous. No further flying took place that day.

13

SOME RIVERSIDE BOATING CENTRES

Traditionally, much more use was made of the Stour's southern extremity, then in Hampshire, than the Dorset stretches, both for salmon, sailing and tea gardens.

Tuckton Creeks (1903-1921)   W. Nutter Scott, Proprietor.

Iford Bridge Boating (1907-c.1925).   The establishment of George Rogers. Elliott took
house (+ tennis). Another existed nearby.   over the business in March 1907.

Wick Ferry Tea Boat (1908 - ?).   J.C. Edmunds c.1903 then the Misses Alder.

Riverside Cottage Tea House (1909-14).   Teas only 1/3d including boat hire.

French Gardens - Stour Road (1911+).   See also, River of Pleasure <u>Bournemouth</u>
Tuckton Bridge. N. side). Teas   <u>Guardian</u> 12.8.1911.
(See <u>Bournemouth Graphic</u> 24.3.1911).

Mudeford Spit. Teaboat and Jetty
(Harbourside) 1920+.

Wick Ferry Riverside Camp & Restaurant   J.C. Edmunds (prop).   See below.

Old Waterworks Teahouse. H.W. Kiddle   This site was originally the printing house of the
proprietor. (boating, picnic parties, teas &c) Russian emigress led by Count Chertkov.
(1921+). Kiddle came from near
Mappowder, Dorset.

Newlyn & Ball (ex Tuckton Creeks).   "Lookout for the purple and gold flag". Soon a
(1923 to 1939)   rendezvous for bridge drives c.1928. (See
    <u>Bournemouth Graphic</u> op. 30.3.1923.)

Note: After the Second World War, Newlyn & Ball's site was owned by a man named Walton
and then (before Bournemouth Boating Services) by a man named Lowe.

McArdles self-service holiday camp (near   The original boathouse 1906+ was replaced after
Wick Ferry) and Wick Ferry Restaurant.   the war by a breezeblock long house; the cabins
(1953+)   replacing earlier 1930's wooden ones behind.
J. Warner (Wick House) (c.1958).   Further development came under Warner and
Pontins Holiday Camp (1963).   Pontin.

Marine Auctions (Tuckton).   Finally demolished in January 1985.

Bournemouth Boating Services.   Messrs. Elliott & Robin Stride who in 1985 ran
    4 boats.

See also <u>Bournemouth Times</u>, 3.8.1934, A History of the Stour.

THE FERRY TEA BOAT.

Under entirely new management and personal direction of the MISSES ALDER.

NEAR THE PRIORY. CHRISTCHURCH. AND SOUTHBOURNE-ON-SEA.

On the prettiest part of River Stour at WICK FERRY.

View of Christchurch Priory from Balcony Tuckton Creeks. Southbourne. Bournemouth.

Tuckton Creeks on the Stour. Southbourne. Bournemouth.

14

RIVER IMPROVEMENTS

The first considerable works on Christchurch Harbour since the abortive schemes of Smeaton, Armstrong & Sylvester (1836) came in the late 1930's, in conjunction with concern over the continuing coastal erosion and the deteriorating state of Mudeford Spit Gradually the Stour had become less and less navigable - once it was possible to get up easily as far as Blandford - and river weeds too, especially above Wick and Tuckton, had rendered it less and less attractive for Salmon. But the decision, in effect to canalize the lower stretches, met with opposition (including from the Druitts in Christchurch) even though the work went ahead, probably to completely destroy the Roman Ford near Double Dykes by so doing. (Pressure for the new works began in 1932 including a planned breach of the spit "to provide a readier outflow.")

viz. 1937: New Channel for Christchurch Harbour.
19 ton dredger at work.

First will be undertaken the removal of the curves and shoals between Christchurch and the under part of the harbour below 'Steepbanks'. The flow of the water at this point is hindered by what is known as Branders Bank, which formed the mid river section of the old Roman ford, Ytinga, which reached from Grimery Point to the old barn which is situated under the ancient earthworks, Double Dykes, on Hengistbury Head.

A deep channel is to be cut through the centre of Branders Bank and to stabilize this course Grimery Point and part of 'Smugglers Island' which lies on the south east of 'Steepbanks' will be cut away.

The plan was to use the 'Priestman Tiger' - a dredger of 19 tons. Mounted on tractors it could move on land whilst, for river use, it was mounted on a giant pontoon.

After 5 months, the dredger was to remove Wick Shoals - the shallows at Wick Ferry.

Bournemouth Times 5.3.1937

Good dredging progress in Christchurch Harbour.

Some 15,000 tons has been dredged. The dredger can be seen from Quomp's Quay. The material was used mainly to form a path across Stanpit Marshes (and to build up the edge of the Marsh). We expect the water level to go down 5-6".

Bournemouth Times 4.6.1937

Note: There had been some dredging at Grimbury in March 1890.

How successful the Priestman Tiger's work was to prove in the long term remains debateable. By 1954, the first steps had to be taken in a large scale investigation "to see if conditions in Christchurch Harbour could be improved". W.H. Crocker, Chief Engineer of the Avon & Dorset Water Board was to make a survey, particularly with regard to concern over a general silting up and consequent damage to the fisheries - something made more urgent when the sea-spit at Mudeford was breached during the great November storm.

In the same year, it was noted also how the upper reaches of the Avon had "not been dredged for over 20 years" with the result that a shoal had developed downstream of Waterloo Bridge, Christchurch.

Most of the Harbour problems it was seen, stemmed from the associated massive coastal erosion, active from the mid 19thC and detailed below.

Wick Village. Christchurch.

Priory from Wick Ferry. Christchurch

15

AN EROSION CHRONOLOGY

In 1869 it was stated that Druitt had known Christchurch Head from 1838 "before which time no changes had been perceptible in the space of twenty years, when it was defended by a large ledge, and also a barrier of iron-stone boulders...but since 1848, at which time excavations were made by a mining company, and large quantities of this stone removed, the waste had been considerable, as much as eight acres in a mile of frontage. In 1851, the late Sir G.H. Rose called the attention of the Admiralty to the damage being perpetrated on our coast by the removal of the ironstone, and in 1854, Capt. Vetch was sent to make an inspection and hold an enquiry into the subject, and the result was the stoppage of the excavation for the iron-stone. Since then however, no action had been taken by the Admiralty and the danger was increasing."

March 1869	Druitt speaks out on the rapid and damaging erosion at Hengistbury Head. He notes that from an 1843 map - the extreme N/S width of the Head was once over 800 yards. Schemes considered include an artificial cut at Double Dykes.
Summer 1870	During Summer 1870, a final halt was called to the ironstone mining on and around Warren - most probably as a result of pressure (on the Board of Trade officials) from influential Bournemouth and other residents. (See Ironstone Canyon 1986)
January 1873	A letter from the Board of Trade notes that it has no objection to a cut being made in the growing Sandbank at Mudeford. This had formed, it said, in the last 6-8 years and was now reaching to Highcliffe Castle, preventing fishermen and traders getting up river to Christchurch.
November 1876	A heavy storm ravages the coast and 'Western shore'. Bournemouth pier loses 60' of its length.
November 1877	A local correspondent noted the damage around Double Dykes and thought a few more winters would see the waters pass right through. Should the rivers be allowed to run out at Double Ditches?
December 1881	The 'entrance' to the Harbour near Mudeford gives serious trouble - being periodically 'blocked'. Breaches will now occur regularly henceforth.
January 1884	The sea breaks over Mudeford Spit in severe gales.

Nov./Dec. 1884	Extension railway plans - involving a huge dock below Warren are outlined - together with a 'cut' at Double Dykes.
March 1885	In defiance of the weather evidence, a pier is proposed for Southbourne.
September 1885	The undercliff parade is opened at Southbourne (Thursday 24.9.1885).
December 1886	A 'Hurricane' is reported locally.
August 1888	Southbourne Pier opens (Mon. 6.8.1888).
September 1888	Bournemouth steamers neglect Southbourne Pier.
January 1890	A gale washes away part of the Southbourne esplanade plus the wooden breakwater. A considerable portion of the cliff founders.
Jan./Feb. 1892	Considerable new fears are expressed about the deteriorating condition of the headland. 'Druitt's deluge' is remembered. "Will Christchurch be deluged and when?" Whitepit - near Double Dykes, gives most concern.
March 1894	The pier approach at Southbourne is to be re-erected. The sea wall has been fractured since February 1892.
December 1898	A terrific gale in the Channel. The Marie Therese is wrecked below Warren.
March 1899	The Marie Therese effects are sold insitu.
Summer 1900	The military blow up the remains of the wreck of the Marie Therese as a practice exercise but much remains.
October 1900	The 'waste of the cliffs' at Warren is estimated at some 500 ft since 1840. (N/S).
March 1901	Death of J.E. Holloway, the man responsible. (30.3.1901).
May 1901	Lecture on Christchurch Head by George Brownen at Double Dykes. He notes how the Romans had worked the ironstone but that the most considerable damage had been done in the last 60 years. The cliffs continued to founder relentlessly.
July 1904	Death of Ald. James Druitt (aged 88).
December 1904	Death of Frederick Derham, another long term local opponent of the ironstone extraction (aged 78). The Mudeford sandbank continues to grow and to thicken in the lee of the headland.

December 1906	More reports circulate as a result of a B. of T. enquiry into national coast erosion. There is known to be continued undermining not only of the exposed western shore, below Warren, but at Highcliffe also. Armstrong's 1836 report is reprinted and now comes the first scheme for a 'new' ironstone groyne to protect the headland.
July 1907	The local erosion of the cliffs provokes a local meeting and yet more concern - especially over the really vulnerable portion near Double Dykes.
November 1907	The first report of the Royal Commissioners - their Blue Book - is published. It is noted how "only small draught vessels can get into Christchurch Harbour" now since the entrance has been carried east $1\frac{1}{2}$ miles. John Druitt (Town Clerk).
February 1908	Another great gale visits the coast, the worst since the 19thC's worst of 24.3.1894.
1909	**The Clifftop** Early days in Southbourne - when the cliffs were sand dunes. There were only two means of access to the beach there in 1909; Fisherman's Walk and Gordon Steps (long wooden steps angular to the cliffs). The Overcliff drive was hardly thought of and instead nothing but high sand dunes extended from Boscombe to Southbourne. This was gradually levelled and replaced by turf and mesembryanthemum. Boscombe to Pokesdown Cliffs was mainly in private ownership with the Gordon Steps "an Alpine climb." **Origin of Fishermen's Walk** "There was, at one time, no road to the sea in that neighbourhood, and as Mackerel fishing was carried on extensively, especially by fishermen from Poole, the men used to make a short cut through the pines and brushwood to the village inn. In this way a path came to be formed by continual use not only by the fishermen but by the general public and eventually Lord Portman and Mr. Curling Hunter who owned the woods were approached to give up a strip of land to make a proper public path. After the completion of negotiations, the Local Authority made the path through to the cliff and wooden steps were erected to give access to the beach."
Summer 1909	The "old picturesqueness" of the East side of Fisherman's Walk gives way to a building estate.
September 1910	More correspondence on coast erosion and renewed fears of an irruption at Double Dykes.
Winter 1911	The Sandbar is breached by a gale at the 'Run' end.

October 1916	More gales and more floods locally.
November 1916	The quay at Christchurch is flooded - many say a situation made worse by the long Sandbar at Mudeford impounding the waters.
December 1916	F.P. Dolamore, Bournemouth Borough Engineer notes the recent gale (5th November) has destroyed both Gordon Steps and Joseph Steps, with the waste of the Southbourne coast since 1909 between 35 and 64 feet.
Jan./March 1918	Arthur Pullman of Sea Croft, Cliff Drive, complains repeatedly of the neglect by Bournemouth of Southbourne. He notes the high rate of attrition of the cliffs and the parlous condition of the place he attributes to the resorts "masterly inactivity"; their "conspiracy of silence."
May 1921	Dolamore omits Southbourne from announced urgent coastal defensive works.
March 1923	More serious floods occur at Christchurch.
January 1925	The Gordon Steps now provide "the only means of access between Fisherman's Walk and Sea Road whilst there is no proper beach access at Southbourne.
	Towards the end of this month, in another great gale, the last part of the sea wall at Southbourne was "smashed to pieces". It had been a block 20 ft long and 10 ft high and had stood out the longest. After this, "the only bit left standing (was) a flight of steps that takes you nowhere."
March 1925	A seawall is to be made at Fisherman's Walk - forming an isolated terrace; Today it is another quirk in today's 5 mile linear tapestry.
February 1926	More questions are asked about the struggle to get hold of Southbourne Beach. Capt. A.W. Phillips states he has been fighting to secure Council ownership for over 20 years and wants - at all costs - to avoid bungalow development along the cliff top.
	Again the very real danger of a massive inroad of the sea near Double Dykes is noted making Hengistbury an island and Christchurch a seaside resort. C.E. Smith's monument has had to be moved again.
January 1928	The receding cliffs at Southbourne continue to worry local residents. Meantime Bournemouth Council try to gain control of the cliff and beach which are still in private ownership - a Company represented by A. Curling Hunter (then in Cannes - and "likely to be there some time") controls this. There are fears for 'Sea Croft' which is now very close to the cliff edge and pleas for timber groynes and a zig zag path to Crossroads (first suggested in 1925). Apparently the sea had

encroached tremendously at Cellars Farm in the past few years whilst the Gordon Steps (the latest made in 1926) showed a 20 yard loss in 12 years. Curling Hunter owned all the beach and clifftop from Gordon Steps to Hengistbury Head having given Bournemouth, Fisherman's Walk to Gordon Steps earlier.

February 1928	There are improvements at Fisherman's Walk where the landmark beach kiosk, on its little promenade, is to be converted to a public shelter - a nearby refreshment hut to be enlarged.
	For those interested, a walk along the Bournemouth promenade today, can still reveal the complex evolution of the coast protection works - or their absence marked by periodic embayments.
March 1928	Talks with A.C. Hunter continue re problems of beach access at Southbourne.
April 1928	Despite 1180 petition signatories, no lift is to be made near Fisherman's Walk. The E. & W. lifts at Bournemouth date to 1905 and cost £4,000 each.
November 1931	A large part of Southbourne's coast road falls into the sea.
March 1932	Worries continue about the serious wastage of the Head. There are plans to breach Mudeford Spit to get a better outflow and to prevent flooding.
November 1932	Once Bournemouth Council obtained control of the Headland, the Borough Engineer was instructed "to make a better safeguard against wind and waves". Quite soon the construction of a "massive groyne" was said to be favoured.
January 1933	Canute's Chair, last vestige of Southbourne Pier, tumbles.
February 1935	There are strong objections to building clifftop homes which "spoil the view at the eastern end of the front" - i.e., to Solent Road. General Austin said "as a result of the lack of attention to the eastern area in the past, the land on the seafront east of the Gordon Hotel to Hengistbury Head fell into the hands of private owners" which proved "a thorn in the flesh" to the Corporation over the years. Fortunately it was thought the new Town Planning scheme would put an end to further cliff top building and so stop Southbourne being walled up by private speculators.
March 1935	A new 'gap' appears in Mudeford Spit.
June 1935	The new £7,000 cliff lift opens at Fishernman's Walk (8th).

September 1935	Historic gale (on Mon. 16th) changes the coast's contours, especially at Mudeford.
December 1935	Death of Mrs. M.R. Compton - the widow of Southbourne's pioneer - at 'Sea View', St. Catherine's Road. Aged 93.
January 1936	More pleas for new erosion prevention works at Hengistbury.
February 1936	Southbourne still lacks Bournemouth's attention. It is seen as the 'cinderella' of the family. Meantime caravans and tents are pitched every Summer near Dalmeny Road and the coastguards giving the place a bohemian 'feel'.
March 1936	Alarm is expressed over the continuing erosion rate. House gardens now approach the cliff edge while the Overcliff Steps are half destroyed in cliff falls. F.P. Dolamore, Borough Engineer for 20 years, retires.
July 1936	Arthur Bedford buys the beach at Southbourne. He plans to develop the 1 mile frontage in the interests of the locale.
September 1936	More statistics are published on the damage done by the ironstone extractions (1848-70).
December 1936	Extensive sand dune removal (5,000 tons) takes place prior to constructing the £1,850 Fisherman's Walk - sunken ornamental garden. They open this year. Erosion statistics for the coast to this time were: 18 feet p.a. during the ironstone mining years 1848-70; $2\frac{1}{2}$ p.a. 1871-96; 4 ft p.a. 1897-1907, and $1\frac{1}{2}$ ft p.a. 1908-36.

January 1937

The New Groyne

There was now under construction a Light Railway around the eastern point of Hengistbury Head, over a mile in length and used to convey material for the construction of the £19,000 Sea Groyne which was planned to extend over 700' seaward.

The Light Railway was planned to convey the hundreds of tons of cement and steel rails needed as the work progressed. A base of concrete was erected of about 17' in width in large containers of canvas stiffened with old Bournemouth tramlines to give rigidity.

Note: W.L. Clowes was the Bournemouth Borough Engineer in charge of the works. The original idea is said to have come from his predecessor F.P. Dolamore and the main problem (finally baulked at) was to 'bridge the Deep' to the Beerpans rocks.

Interestingly, the long groyne was used in the 2nd World War for on and off-loading of supplies - so providing Christchurch at last with a sort of port outlet on the sea.

March 1937	Associated River dredging by the Priestman Tiger continues.
April 1937	Herbert Druitt writes about his fears of the effects of the rivers' canalisation.
September 1937	Already the sand was said to be building up by the new Long Groyne and on the Mudeford side. Erosion statistics given were 18' lost p.a. 1850-70 and 1½ feet p.a. 1900-36. Fine weather in mid 1937 allowed good progress to be made with construction, even though a further 2 years' work was envisaged. A huge derrick was involved at the groyne end served by the diesel oil loco "Bournemouth Belle". Old tram lines were sunk in the base of the groyne.
January 1939	Hengistbury Groyne is reported a success but generally, erosion at Southbourne is still considered 'a crisis'.
March 1944	There are plans to develop Christchurch Harbour as a yachting centre after the war and for new protective groynes at Avon Beach.
March 1946	Southbourne coast erosion brings a pill-box to the shore at Bedford beach.
February 1947	Overcliff Gardens at Southbourne are reported to be "vanishing".
November 1954	In the great storm (the worst for over 20 years) of 27th November, the Sandspit at Hengistbury Head was breached with consequent flooding in the harbour. Plans begin for permanent sea defence works here. (See Mudeford entries.)
December 1954	Cliff top families 'in terror' on Southbourne Cliff Drive following "huge erosion" in the wake of the great storm - the worst for 20 years (27.11.1954). The road had collapsed already.
	Tuckton traders have monthly meetings at the Tea Gardens. Soon action includes the building of the steel barrier below the cliff Drive, Southbourne. The Southbourne Cliff Drive is no more.
August 1955	Just 10 houses remain on the Southbourne overstrand now - protected by these new 'iron' defences.
March 1956	Arthur Bedford sells his 'Bedford Beach' (which he had bought in 1936 from A. Curling Hunter, liquidator of Rugbey Ltd) to Bournemouth Council. Bedford carried out extensive sea defence works at this Southbourne site - from the old pier promenade to Solent Road. Fortes - the present renters of the cafe, were to continue for the year.

April 1956	A new lease is arranged for Canute! Cafe which had been built in 1937 but had not been used - on its highly exposed site - since the War. It would now linger on - for many years.
May 1956	The Art Deco houses in danger on Southbourne Overcliffe are to be bought by the Corporation. Erosion has now moved to within 2-3 paces of their backdoors (viz. No's 136-140). No. 136 was built 1932-4 despite big cliff falls in 1933-4. No. 140 lost 30 feet of its garden in the disastrous gale of 1950. 10 houses would go altogether with 136-142 the first. They can be seen hovering at the cliff edge in postcards of the period whilst today, only a dozen yards of their plots remain by the roadside. This history explains today's roadnet.
February 1957	Work proceeds fast on the demolition of these threatened cliff top houses.
April 1959	George Howard's 'Shell House' regains its earlier solitude as almost the sole (first) house on this part of the cliff top.
January 1960	There is severe storm damage to the seafront of 'Bedford's Beach.'
November 1963	Another storm breaks over 'Bedford's Beach' - waves overtop the cafe.
Spring 1966	An extensive and rare sea thrift colony establishes itself on the clifftop near Harbour Road.
Early 1970's	As funds became available - so 'Bedford Beach' was remodelled and reformed, new groynes put in place and the remnants of the old promenade (the rocks) gradually largely removed. Soon a new overcliff drive would obliterate most of the old Southbourne features even as the coast here was stabilised. Erosion, behind the promenades at least, seems to have come to an end.
January 1987	Report on the deteriorating condition of the Head. A 77 page management plan is published.
1990-2	Massive sea defence works continue.
October 1992	New Mudeford/Haven Quay sea protection works are in prospect in response to sea wall undermining and fears of global warming's effects.

LAND SALES IN THE 20th C   16

It mustn't be forgotten how wild and exposed the Western Shore and its empty lands out towards Hengistbury were, even at the turn of the century. The river seemed as good a way as any by which to visit it in Summer and only Broadway Lane ran across the plateau, joining the famous smuggling track up from Wick Village. There was no bus route and no

Broadway and no building though Broom Close (today's Library) set an attractive precedent in 1908; the Well House in Wick in the same year.

Accordingly, it's no surprise to see how building development clung closely to Tuckton and its approaches or was concentrated on further infilling at Southbourne including the attractive St. Katharine's Road despite the Land Companies' difficulties. There were projects for the empty zone however, no doubt stimulated by the realization of the beauty of the site following the air pageant and all seem to have taken renewed life when Christchurch, not Bournemouth, unexpectedly secured Hengistbury Head within its boundaries (Winter 1911). At once, there was canvassed the feared project of bungalow development and up to Warren, once the land had been secured finally from Sir George Meyrick.

But, as later, war intervened and it was to be Gordon Selfridge a resident now at Highcliffe Castle (from Nov. 1916) who successfully bought not only Hengistbury but a lot of the surrounding land including substantial lots at Stanpit and in Wick. This, at least, served to freeze further planned assaults on the main area until 1930 (but see Appendix) with the result housebuilding - for the forthcoming great decades - would go elsewhere, i.e., to Iford, Cranleigh, Tuckton and surrounds. In particular, the lands west of Tuckton began to fill up in the 1920's as the urban army began to flow down from Foxholes Wood (destroying the ancient fort in the process) and these soon followed by the Dean's sale of the Iford Estate, announced periodically from June 1923. This was followed quickly by 80 plots on the Cellars Farm Estate (in August 1923; i.e. around Hengistbury Road and Dalmeny Avenue) whilst, during the next year (August 1924) considerable land was sold in and around Wick where Brightlands and Riverlands Estates "situate in well constructed avenues" and 54 plots in all, were sold by Auction in July 1925, more following the next season. Freehold building land (24 plots) was also disposed of "east of Tuckton Bridge" and by 'West Heath', Belle Vue Road. Once isolated Tuckton Farm was sold in June 1926 and more plots in Sunnylands Avenue in 1930. And then (see below) came the great sale by Selfridge, of Hengistbury Head that August being, fortuitously and just in time, bought by Bournemouth Corporation who, henceforth vowed to preserve it if not the plateau below - poetically named Solent Meads. But this was all quite an encouraging sign for the future - the building line not yet so irrevocably far advanced until just before the Second World War when the Broadway and then the Saxon King Hotel (1940) provided the all important stimulus long denied. Soon the real masses might be able to descend.

OVER-CLIFF DRIVE, SOUTHBOURNE.

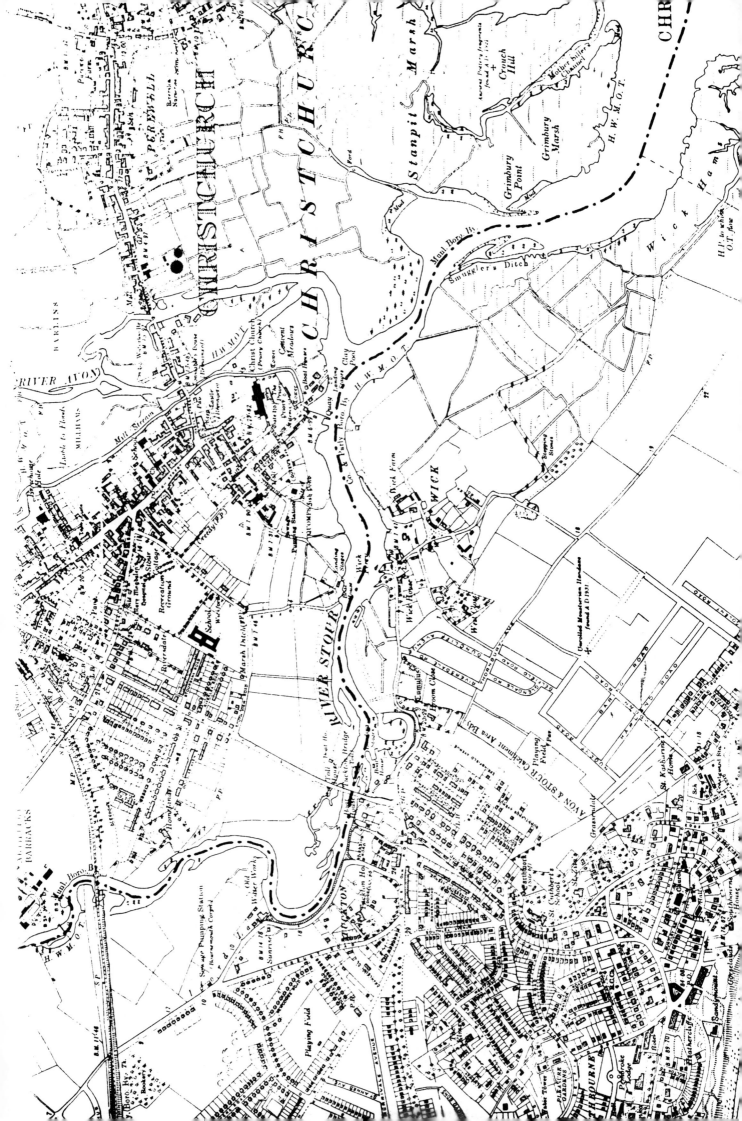

Summer 1902   Southbourne on Sea Building Estate (Druitts: Solicitors).

January 1911   Heatherlea property (Tuckton) sold.

November 1911   A prospect of development at Hengistbury Head by bungalows is mooted.   Christchurch Town Council (despite opposition from Bournemouth) extends its boundaries to include Hengistbury Head. The important change of ownership from Sir George Meyrick, was to "shortly come into effect."

1915-1916	Gordon Selfridge buys Hengistbury Head plus surrounding lands and including some at Stanpit and Wick. Selfridge had been living at Highcliffe Castle since November 1916.
June 1923	Sale of Iford Estate.
August 1923	Sale of Cellars Farm Estate (80 plots). These lay mainly around already developing Hengistbury Road and Dalmeny Avenue.
August 1924	Wick land sales.
July 1925	Estates for sale ("situate in well constructed avenues") i.e. Brightlands and Riverlands. 54 plots by auction. 800 new houses will be built in Bournemouth this year.
November 1925	55 plots are offered on the Carbery Estate - adjoining Southbourne Grove. They are situated in Carbery Avenue (45' x 160'), Watcombe and Seafield Roads.
December 1925	Another 79 plots are sold at auction on the Carbery Estate. "Demand was hardly less diminished" with "spirited bidding". Sites too, were on sale in Cranleigh Road - once called "half-way lane".
Summer 1926	Wick Lane auction. Further plots are sold in Broadlands and Southlands Avenues. Also considerable land sales continue around Tuckton, Cranleigh and Carbery.
June 1926	Tuckton Farm sale. A farmhouse and 11 shop sites. The sale was held on Mon. 7.6.1926 at 3.00 p.m. The tithe boundary passed between plots 8 and 9.
September 1926	More land sales at Iford, on the Cooper Dean land.
July 1930	Freehold building land. Southbourne on Sea. 24 sites east of Tuckton Bridge and 'West Heath', Belle Vue Road. (Willow Way plots). Also Sunnylands Ave., plots 138-170. Others for sale near Belle Vue Road and St. Katharine's Road.
August 1930	Hengistbury Head (The sale held at Bournemouth Town Hall) comprising 700 acres, including lands at Wick and on the approaches to the headland. (see below.)
October 1931	Building estate at Iford Lane.
April 1933	Wick Lane development.
Summer 1935	Broadway opened - making the entire Headland, at once, more accessible to the general public. Buses were soon in operation.

September 1936	1500 plots now sold on the Iford Estate and 120 since April.
April 1938	Opposition grows to further building out towards Hengistbury Head.
February 1939	The Saxon King Hotel plan, a large roadhouse halfway down the new Broadway, is approved while debate grows over the provision of a cafe at Double Dykes.

HENGISTBURY HEAD SALE

By direction of Gordon Selfridge Esq., Hampshire.
The Hengistbury Head Estate   6.8.1930
Sols: Stephenson, Harwood & Tatham
Auctioneers: Messrs Knight, Frank & Rutley

Lot 1	Hengistbury Head, Warren Hill and Double Dykes. 231 Acres.
Lot 2	Wick Farm (Tenant W.R. Carter). 191 Acres.
Lot 6	Note: Crooked Oak Cottage occupied by W.R. Burry (Lot 6).
Lot 8	Wick Meads (i.e. Sanctuary) Accommodation Grass field.
Note:	Plots 15-19 include the gravel pit by Wick Lane up as far as Broadway Lane - today's Thornbury Road. Harbour Road - running past the future (1939) Saxon King site was known as Cellars Lane.

Lots 15-19 were described as:

"An important area of land with a valuable gravel pit occupying a good position just south of Wick village with about 970' of road frontage and commanding fine views over Hengistbury Head and Christchurch Harbour. (4.6 acres).

They are let with Wick Farm on a yearly (Michaelmas) tenancy to Mr. W.R. Carter who is quitting at Michaelmas 1930.

If not sold as a whole, the lots will be offered separately."

Restrictive covenants re. building are imposed by Selfridge.

AROUND CHRISTCHURCH

July 1904	Death of Alderman James Druitt (84).
August 1914	Opening of the Union Jack Club. It continued in operation well after 1918.

August 1916	There are pleas locally to make the muddy fields at Quomps into a pleasure ground.
1914-1918	No defensive works are known around Christchurch during the first war - not even a harbour guardship, but large numbers of wounded soldiers were treated in the area whilst troop manouevres - as in 1915 on Hengistbury - were widespread and commonplace.
1928	There are attempts to get Place mill on the Quay made the subject of a Preservation Order. Apparently the lower (stone) portion of the walling "dates before the Reformation" with 16-17thC brickwork above and a late 18thC roof.
1932	Extensive land sales take place around Friars Cliff (87 plots).
September 1935	There are pleas to protect and preserve the threatened Norman House at the bridge. Will it be cleared of ivy?
February 1936	Christchurch prepares itself for the arrival of trolley buses. The turning point for the new vehicles is being 'negotiated'
April 1936	'Good Riddance' to the last tramcars (Wed. 8th). The first trolley ran over Tuckton Bridge on the 8th. Tolls continue, however.
September 1939	There is an auction sale of Hengistbury House and gardeners cottage at 35 Purewell.

(Note: March 1947   The Norman House is cleared of ivy and the spiral staircase revealed.)

Licensed hotel near Hengistbury Head

'Application for a provisional licence for a new hotel in the Hengistbury Head district was granted at Bournemouth annual licensing sessions on Wednesday 8th February.

The hotel is to be erected by Messrs. Eldridge Pope & Co in Cellars Lane and is to be called 'the Saxon King'.

Mr. F.E. Pilcher for the applicant said there were 284 houses in the area, only 28 of which were unoccupied and a large number of visitors went to the district.

The proposed hotel would have 14 bedrooms, 9 of which would be for letting, a tea garden and a children's garden.

Mr. W.F. Ruther, opposing on behalf of residents said that the district might tend to be spoilt by the erection of licensed premises. Further the number of houses in the district did not justify the application which he submitted was premature.

The Chairman (Mr. G.C. Guest) announced that the monopoly question was settled and satisfactory.
A monetary value of £4,000 for an annual license was agreed Bournemouth Times, 10.2.1939

Note: The Saxon King opened on 6th February 1940 and closed on Sunday, 19th July 1992.

Although there was disquiet at the rate of development from 1938, it took until 1954 for a campaign to develop.

Early March 1954   A proposed development of over 56 Acres "on either side of the Broadway", on which 4 to 500 houses may be built, appeared in the Town & Country Development Plan. The area to be built on ran out as far as the Double Dykes; to the coast on the south side and the edge of the marshland on the north. A fierce correspondence followed the announcement.

A week later this "battle for the ancient Channel port of Hengistbury Head" took a new turn when 2 new local residents associations moved to oppose the building scheme. They crossed swords over the best method of blocking the proposed housing development. 200 people packed Tuckton Tea Gardens. The main weapon of the Hengistbury Head Residents Association was a massive petition. Their Chairman J.W. Maycock asserted "the loss of any part of this natural playground for housing development would be a disaster of the first magnitude." As an alternative he suggested the Council turn their attention to the "provision of gardens, parks, playing fields and recreation grounds which would preserve the open character of the area...as a permanent asset to the town."

Councillor Derick Scott gave a short history of the plots, saying the Council bought the site for £25,250 in 1930. It was always their intention to develop parts of it but their earlier plans were affected by the war. Most of it was now farmland but the lease expired in 1956. Covenants in 1930 said no more than 10 houses should be built per acre at £1,000 each.

Late March 1954   Arthur Bedford proposed to build 10 tudor style shops just west of the Saxon King. He was also to sell 150 bungalow plots bounded by the Broadway, Belfield Avenue, Thornbury Road and the Saxon King.

There was also a threat that the land leading up to Double Dykes would be sold. Local rate payers voted to oppose any more houses east of the Saxon King.

April 1954   Tuckton traders meanwhile, opposed this plan to build shops along the Broadway together with a petrol station. It was said that "if private houses had not been built there, there would have been 'a sewage farm, airfield and council houses'.

As Bournemouth Council appeared to be winning, the HRA determine to carry the fight to Whitehall. 5000 signed the petition against the housing development. Meanwhile there was the decision of the Housing Committee to build blocks of 2 storey flats on the Broom Close site.

A 'Save Hengistbury Head' plea was made to the Minister Harold MacMillan. Nigel Nicolson MP backed the HRA.

May 1954   Broom Close. Another change of plan in Wick Lane when the idea for flats is rejected. A possible Old Folks Home was substituted, for the grounds. It was reported Broom Close House (now Tuckton Library) was requisitioned by the Military during the Second World War and after that, the Welfare Services Committee considered using it as a place for old people if a new wing were added. All the time, on the land around, new bungalow dwellings were springing up where once were fields and briefly the canvas hangars of the air pageant (1910) contestants.

July 1954   A further step is taken re the disposal of the land at Hengistbury. It is to be known as the Solent Meads Estate and to all be used for bungalows or semi-bungalows.

September 1954   The Bournemouth Development plan includes a scheme for a Riverside Walk following the water's edge by Iford Lane - at the foot of the 'river cliff'.

March 1955   'Sale recalls Hengistbury battle'. The sale of 23 plots on the Solent Meads Estate is to take place in April with building restricted to bungalows and semis. The plots face Broadway and Harbour Road and are to be sold individually. Following the 'battle' in 1954, the Council "finally decided to allow development up to the Saxon King and Double Dykes but not of the Head itself."

April 1955   'Top prices' are reported paid at the Hengistbury Head Auction. The 23 lots go for £17,210 in the sale, held at the Saxon King. Local people and building firms were prominent. The next auction is set for September 1955 i.e., for the lands East of the Saxon King out to Double Dykes.

March 1956   The Broadway shops are to open soon.

March 1957   There is a 'shadow' over Mrs. S. Barber's house, 1 Solent Road - as the Council planned a car park on the nearby Solent Meads Estate. The Barbers had owned the house since the mid 1930's. (It was demolished finally in 1991.)

May 1958	Report on the Solent Meads sale. 26 plots sold by auction on Wed. 28th May. (One unnamed site was the new disintegrator sewage pumping station.) Clowes Avenue, (120') the widest in Bournemouth - contained the majority of the plots. It was said to be the largest and last development sale in Bournemouth, £23,575 (26 plots). It was expected there would be 3 or 4 more sales on the Solent Meads Estate.
July 1958	"The pre-war look" slowly returns to Hengistbury as demolition progresses on wartime defence works. "Gone is the huge concrete blockhouse which marred the view from the refreshment rooms. Going are the gun emplacements, bunkers, radar installations, Nissen Huts and anti-tank "dragons teeth". Bournemouth Corporation expected to complete the clearance by early 1959.
March 1959	'Clowes Avenue' deliberately made one of the 3 finest in Bournemouth to increase value of adjoining land. 200 Solent Meads plots remain.

DEMOLITION OF THE SAXON KING

The pub closed in Summer 1992 (Sunday 19.7.92).

Demolition began in late August - first the building was fenced off and nothing much happened for a week.

The 'lads' made one last protest, building a float of remembrance RIP Saxon King and paraded noisily in it one weekend.

I photographed demolition work - first 'off' the roof, 1-8th September 1992.
Blue tile - by request. ? Italian.

Most of the shell (except the roof) was there to 11.9.92 (Friday), but 2 o'clock on Saturday afternoon (12th) a JCB type machine pushed the walls in and destroyed the Public Bar about 3.00 p.m. My photographs 20-25 refer. (12.9.92).

I photographed the very last bit of wall being demolished at 5.15 p.m. on Monday 14.9.92 and at 5.30 p.m. I took a set of the demolition man x 2 (No's. 30-34 on my film).

From Tues. 15.9.92 to 22.9.92 lots of rubble was dug up and carted from the site and the foundations ditto. The huge cellar seems to have been the only one. Garages demolished this week also. No pictures.

28-30th September. Digging footings and laying concrete foundations.
Adverts cover demolition on 1.10.92 and continues 6.10.92. No photographs taken yet.

19.10.92. Still no further on with Broadway side footings - lots of rain - but drainage and little service road put in.

5.11.92. First house half up at shops end and lots of activity.

25.11.92   First house roof timbers go up next to shops.   Photographed   2.12.92 in a
........great storm. 1 roof tiled. 2nd house almost ready for roof 7.12.92.

5.1.93 3 houses near shops almost built. RAIN.

26.1.93   Despite rain and gales, 5 houses facing Broadway have roofs.

8.2.93 Front 5 houses complete. 2nd row in process.

3.3.93 The front row of houses is complete and the 2nd row up to roof level. 'Bungalows'
half done.

APPENDIX 1

LOCAL SEVERE WEATHER

1739-40	A severe 9 week frost.
Winter 1753-54	17° frost.
Winter 1762-63	Thames froze over 1m frost.
Winter 1789	Poole Harbour frozen over.
Winter 1813-1814	Severe Winter. 20" snow Plymouth. Icebergs in Solway.
Winter 1836	Heavy blizzards.
Winter 1838	Poole Harbour frozen over.
1842	The 'Little Ice Age' in U.K. comes to an end. Records begin London 1841.
January 1854	Heavy snowfall.
1860-61	Severe Winter, hard and long frost.
16.1.1864	Good ice sheet at Stanpit, but soon thaws.
*January 1881	3'-8' of snow - all over Christchurch (Christchurch Times 22,1,1881). Streets impassable. Stanpit and shallows of River Stour - all frozen.
January 1884	Gales overtop Mudeford Spit. Rumored wreck off Head.
1896	Poole Harbour frozen over.
1925	June 1925. No rain. Sizzling month.
1940	Severe Winter.
1947	Very severe Winter.
1959	Hot Summer.
1962/3	Christchurch Harbour frozen over. Severe freeze up. Boxing Day - April.

* Christchurch Times
    16.1.1864   "There was a good ice sheet at Stanpit and the venturesome might be seen gliding as far as Blackberry Point". But soon the thaw set in.

APPENDIX 2

POSTCARD PUBLISHERS COVERING SOUTHBOURNE

Aerofilms Series	Hendon, NW9.
Aero Pictorial Ltd	137 Regent Street, London.
Ashfield Series	
Harvey Barton & Son Ltd	Bristol.
Bournemouth View Co.	St. Pauls Lane, Bournemouth.
P.A. Buchanan & Co.	Thornton Heath/Chiswick London.
J.L. Evans	Bournemouth.
F. Frith & Co.	Reigate.
W.G. Hooper	5 The Parade, Crossroads, Southbourne.
Judges Ltd.	Hastings.
Kingsway Real Photo Series	London.
F.S. Kitcher	Cross Roads, Southbourne.
Louis Levy (Sons & Co.)	Paris.

Lofthouse, Crosbie & Co.	London.
J.F. Lovell	Boscombe.
Photochrom Series	London & Tonbridge Wells.
M.J. Ridley	Bournemouth.
Rood Bros.	Southampton.
Rush & Warwick	Bedford.
J. Salmon	Sevenoaks.
Sauls Southbourne Series	
F.G.O. Stuart	Southampton.
Sunray Series	HTB/C&MB.
A. Sutton & Co	3 Southbourne Grove, West Southbourne.
Thunder & Clayden	Bournemouth.
F.W. Todman	Boscombe.
Raphael Tuck & Sons	
Valentine & Sons	Dundee & London.
Wades Sunny South	Bournemouth.
J. Welch & Sons	Portsmouth.
Whittingham	Southbourne.
Woolstone-Barton Co.	London.

POSTCARD PUBLISHERS (HENGISTBURY)

Bournemouth View Co.	St. Pauls Lane, Bournemouth.
J. Clement	Tram Terminus, Christchurch.
Dearden & Wade	Bournemouth.
E.T.W. Dennis & Sons	London & Scarborough.
J.L. Evans	Bournemouth.
Excel Series	
Francis Frith & Co.	Reigate.
Judges Ltd.	Hastings.
Mallett	Christchurch.
Pictorial Stationery Co.	London.
J. Salmon Ltd.	Sevenoaks.
F.G.O. Stuart	Southampton.
E.A. Sweetman & Sons	Tunbridge Wells.
Sydenham & Co.	Bournemouth.
Valentines & Sons	Dundee & London.

POSTCARD PUBLISHERS COVERING MUDEFORD & CHRISTCHURCH

Aero Pictorial Ltd.	Regent Street, London.
J.H. Bishop	Arcade, Bournemouth.
Boots Pelham Series	
Castle Tea House	11 Church Street, Christchurch.
John Davis	Queen Victoria Street, London.
Dearden & Wade	Bournemouth.
Excel Series	
C.W. Faulkner & Co.	
F. Frith & Co.	Reigate.

Gale & Polden Ltd.
W. Hagerberg   London.
Hillier & Co.   Custom House Buildings, Poole.
Holloway & Son   Redcliffe, Bristol.
Judges Ltd.   Hastings.
Lobster Pot Cafe   Mudeford.
Louis Levy (Sons & Co.)   Paris.
Mallett   Christchurch (for Pictorial Stationery Co., London).
George Moss   Christchurch (Photographer).
N.W.J. Nigh   Ventnor, Isle of Wight.
Russell Oakley   Art Publisher, 50 High Street, Christchurch.
Photocrom Co.   London & Tunbridge Wells.
Pictorial Stationery Co.   London.
M.J. Ridley   Bournemouth.
Rush & Warwick   Bedford.
E. & M. Saunders   Christchurch, Hants
Shamrock & Co.   London.
Stengel & Co.   London.
F.G.O. Stuart   Southampton.
Summit Series
Sunray Series   MTB/T&CB.
E.A. Sweetman & Son   Tunbridge Wells.
Thunder & Clayden Series   Bournemouth.
Raphael Tuck & Sons
W. Tucker & Sons   Booksellers, Christchurch.
Valentines Series   Dundee & London.
J. Welch & Sons   Portsmouth.
The Wrench Series
The Wyndham Series

LOCAL ARTISTS

George A. Baker
W.G. Hooper
Sidney Pike
Frank Richards
A.R. Quinton

Selfridge's Castle:

Selfridge's Castle: the Small Castle, from the south.

130

APPENDIX 3

THE LARGEST HOUSE IN THE WORLD

By LAWRENCE POPPLEWELL

What a sight it would have been - floating there in mid sea. And what a palace, a fantasia, like nothing else in England, a colossus in aspect from both sea and mainland. Certainly this headland, Hengistbury, unadorned is impressive enough and in Summer, in a heat haze, it is remote, shimmering; an island almost, of a god - perhaps a Tantalus - a place apart, distinct from the rampart shore of its seaside bay. Ancient moor and heath, ironstone, rock and reef; it was always a dreamplace against a colder reality.

And hence it was here that the creation almost of a rival to Randolph Hearst's St. Simeon came to be built, and for the store-king Gordon Selfridge, had it not been for his money problems developing in the later 1920's, which, to the great relief of our age, finally ended the scheme forever.[1]

He planned it all at Highcliffe Castle (another 'disingenuous chateau')[2] looking out, with Mother, on the Southampton-bound liners bearing his friends from America, and seeing the tawny promontory, the eastern end of which offered the site for the first and smaller of the giant ventures he planned, a lighted house on a sombre shore, a distinctive alternative to the furze and rabbits (of Old Warren Hill), the wrack and wreck and potential coastal ruin - still continuing - which has always been the true leit-motif of this eroding place.

So Selfridge leased the headland on the 11th November, 1916 from Christchurch Council, which authority, after years of struggle against their burgeoning neighbour, first through greedy mineral exploitation and then through local politics, managed finally to 'get their feet in the sea' from 1911 and so stop, at least temporarily, the total Bournemouth annexation of the Bay[3]. No sum is known but the Priory townsfolk, it appears, were glad of a millionaire to hold all the land from them and do as he might with it, both on the hill itself, along the sandspit and, to the west, astride the narrow neck of the connecting isthmus.

And so the incredible was planned with, as architect, Philip Tilden, designer for Churchill of Chartwell in 1922, who, here, in 1919, was summoned to the great man in his Oxford Street store to make a blueprint for this 'largest house in the world'! Comprising castles and ramparts, towers and suites and hundreds of rooms, all spreading for miles around the sandy crumbling crags of this forlorn by beautiful place, it was to separate it forever from its real history. As Tilden saw it.

"The headland was to be fortified against the onslaughts of time by a gigantic wall, punctuated by towers, along its four miles of length and at the tip (of the Head) was to be sheer to the sea a little castle - no larger than Highcliffe - but all a skirt to the real body of the dream (where) high on the plateau (was) planned the larger creation - some sort of useful interpretation of Gothic."[4]

But Gothic horror or fantasy? For months Tilden worked away on the plans, reporting to Selfridge monthly from the 'Moors of Devon', source no doubt for some inspiration from Lipton's newly created Drogo,[5] and also from Balzac who similarly, it was hinted, had "huddled in his own small writing room" to bring forth wonders.[6]

Back and forth to Highcliffe he went, the 64th scale drawings crammed in his portfolio, and here took place endless consultations throughout 1920-21 with the Scottish American from Ulster, the western visionary. So it proceeded always in sections, a piece here a piece there, for the entirety was so enormous and the potential cost incredible. Thus there was to be a main approach from the west, a dual drive sweeping upwards from the flat land beyond the double earthworks of the previous pre-Roman castle builders,[7] and on and on through a massive gateway in the bastioned wall - as if into Toledo - or some such similar Moorish city in Spain. Beyond were to be more stones, vistas, drives, avenues, fountains, piazzas, levels, sea walks, picture galleries, tennis courts, a theatre, ballrooms, and a great hall - "a cloy almost (some thought), of good things."[8]

And at the top, at the very summit of poor sandblown decaying Hengistbury was to be the centrepiece, that incredible Tower, the apex of this English Xanadu. The dome would be only a little less in diameter than St. Paul's but now rising high into the sky to touch the clouds, though The Tower would be climbed by lifts or stairs "to further suites of rooms on every floor for all the visitors of the world". Higher still "studios, laboratories, observatories", and all culminating with "such a roof for view as never was" atop a palace without rival in coastal Europe. It was to be a "cynosure for all eyes", a vulgar meeting place for culture all the world over and, of course, one conveniently close to Southampton.[9]

So in these early 20s, the Anglo-American Beau Monde gathered with Selfridge et al at Highcliffe (previous 'tenants' include the contractor John Aird and Kaiser Wilhelm[10]) to hear the plans for the Head and to view the windblown place on their many Rolls-Royce assisted rambles. Natural features too, it was felt, like 'Blood & Ironstone Canyon'[11], were all to be integrated within the layouts, and hence all felt the incredible was about to arise, an improbable and optimistic legacy for a coast thus exposed.

But still it was all, as Tilden avers, "so nearly realised" and it would have been built had Selfridge not quite so over-stretched himself in money as in years in those golden superficial 20s.[12] Or, like Gatsby, younger perhaps, the essential hollowness of it all may have been beginning to resonate, even though the finale when it came, in 1930 in a local auction room[13] was to be by no means so violent. So the dream remained a dream. Selfridge continued more inward, there were more car and business accidents[14] and perhaps a growing futility. In the end, he sold it all, and the approach and the Wick Village lands he owned, to ever opportunistic but sensible Bournemouth and for just £30,000, forcing Christchurch back from the coast until their later annexation of Avon Beach and Friar's Cliff in 1931[15] with all that has now entailed.

There was one final stipulation, born of money, that the wild place should be preserved as such; a curious paradoxical solution from such a Byzantine giant and his dreams. One ponders often whether he sensed also that time and the 'Brazilian' winds on shore and the erosion of the coast and of nature's other forces too, would have left little, as with graveyards, but tumbled stones, and these just more, yet massive, scribblings on our battered palimpsest.

NOTES

1.   R. Pound, *Selfridge: A Biography*, 1960.
2.   Highcliffe Castle is made up from two large houses in France - the stonework shipped to England between 1830-4. See S.D. Herringshaw, *A Portrait of Highcliffe*, 1987.
3.   See *Bournemouth Graphic*, 24.11.1911 wherein it was first thought that bungalows would be erected on the Head; *Christchurch Times*, 11.11.1916.
4.   P. Tilden, *True Remembrances: The Memoirs of an Architect*, 1954, pp.53-4.
5.   Castle Drogo near Drewsteington is "one of the most remarkable works of Sir Edwin Lutyens." It was begun in 1910 and the plans, part realised only, were similarly expensive and enormous. This 'last country house' built in Britain, dominates the Gorge of the River Teign.
6.   For Balzac, one imagines Bordeaux - not Buckland or Ashburton.
7.   For an intensive study of the archaeology of the Head, see B. Cunliffe, *Hengistbury Head*, 1978.
8.   P. Tilden, p.55.
9.   The transatlantic port, par excellence, of the early 20th C.

10.   For Aird, see *Christchurch Times* 14.11.1899, 18.3.1899 and for the Kaiser, 16 & 23.11.1907, 7.12.1907.

11.   See L. Popplewell, *Ironstone Canyon, The Hengistbury Head Mining Company*, 1986.

12.   Tilden seldom mentions money and never the reason for the end of the scheme, cf R. Pound (Biography).

13.   *Sale Catalogue, Messrs. Knight Frank & Rutley, Hengistbury Head Estate*, (123 Acres) 6th August, 1930. The whole estate comprised 700 acres with Lot 1 (231 acres) being Hengistbury Head and Warren Hill.

14.   See, for example, *Christchurch Times*, 14.10.1916 et seq.

15.   *Christchurch Times and Avon & Friars Cliff Estate Plans*, 1931, (87 plots) see Christchurch Local Collection, Druitt Library.

·AMERICAN LINE·

OUTWARD BOUND
· U.S.M.S.S."ST.LOUIS" PASSING THE NEEDLES.

1884

BIBLIOGRAPHY

J. BARKER	Christchurch Barracks, 1984
B. BARNES	Coast and Shore, 1986
W.G. BEDDINGTON & E.B. CHRISTY	It happened in Hampshire, 1937
N. BELL	From Harbour to Harbour, 1916
G.F. BERKELEY	My Life and Recollections, 1865
LORD BRABAZON	The Brabazon Story, 1956
P. BRANNON	Illustrated, Historical & Pictorial Guide to Bournemouth, 1880
F. BROWNE	Iford, The Last Village, 1974
R.A. COX	The Christchurch Millers Boy, 1974
C. COCHRANE	Poole Bay & Purbeck 1660-1920, 1971
K.M. CHACKSFIELD	Smuggling Days, 1966
T.A. COMPTON	Southbourne's Infancy, 1918
B. CUNLIFFE	Hengistbury Head, 1978
L. DAWSON	Wings over Dorset, Aviation's Story in the South, 1983
G.M. DEAR	From Watermills to Waterworks at Christchurch, 1979
M. DRUITT	Christchurch Miscellany, 1931
T. DYSON	The History of Christchurch, 1955
M. GIROUARD	Mompesson House, 1959
E. GWYNNE JONES	SRDE 1903-1973, 1973
M. HODGES	Prepared for Battle, 1974, 1982
R.M. LOCKLEY	The Private Life of the Rabbit, 1976
C.H. MATE & C. RIDDLE	Bournemouth 1810-1910, 1910
H. MOODY	Sketches of Hampshire, n.d.
E.R. OAKLEY	The Smugglers of Christchurch, BourneHeath & the New Forest, 1944
C.E. PEPIN (ed)	Hengistbury Head, 1979
A.L. PARIS	Christchurch Harbour and the Removal of Ironstone from Hengistbury Head, 1954
F. PONTIN	Thumbs Up, 1991
L. POPPLEWELL	The Largest House in the World, Dorset Year Book, 1988, pp. 78-81
L. POPPLEWELL	Coastguard & Preventive upon the Shipwreck Coast, 1989
M.F. POWELL & J.E. CLARK	Trade & Smuggling in Christchurch, 1982
R. POUND	Selfridge, A Biography, 1960
C.E. ROBINSON	A Royal Warren or Picturesque Rambles in the Isle of Purbeck, 1882
P. TILDEN	True Remembrances: The Memoirs of an Architect, 1954
W. TUCKER	Reminiscences of Christchurch & Neighbourhood, 1920

Victoria County History of Hampshire, Vol. 5, 1912

M.E. WALCOTT	Memorials of Christchurch, 1868
A. WHITE	Christchurch Airfield 1926-1966, 1987

WILLIAM WHITE	Historical Gazetteer and Directory of Hampshire, 1859
E.G. WILLS	Pokesdown & Neighbourhood 1895-1910, 1979
B. WOODWARD & T.C. WILKES	A General History of Hampshire, Vol. 3, 1869
A. YARRANTON	England's Improvements by Land and Sea, 1687
J.A. YOUNG	The Story of Southbourne 1989

LOCAL NEWSPAPERS

BOURNEMOUTH ECHO
BOURNEMOUTH GRAPHIC
BOURNEMOUTH GUARDIAN
BOURNEMOUTH OBSERVER
BOURNEMOUTH TIMES
BOURNEMOUTH VISITORS DIRECTORY
CHRISTCHURCH TIMES
DORSET FREE PRESS

ALSO

HAMPSHIRE COUNTY MAGAZINE, Vol. 1, No. 7, May 1961 (Bathing Belles at Mudeford).
THE EXCELSIOR GUIDE TO CHRISTCHURCH, c.1905.
MARSHALLS DIRECTORY & HANDBOOK OF CHRISTCHURCH, 1913.
THE GRAPHIC GUIDE TO CHRISTCHURCH, (Ed. W.C. Berwick Sayers) n.d.
THE (OFFICIAL) GUIDE TO CHRISTCHURCH, 1933 et seq.

THE WIMBORNE & CHRISTCHURCH RAILWAY PLANS. 4 pieces. (Plans and sections, 1885). A.L. Nimmo and E.W. Ives, Engineers: are contained in the D.C.R.O. Dorchester whilst various maps, including Brights Map of Bournemouth 1884, 1890, 1903 etc. (3" - 1 mile) may be seen locally in the town's reference library. The first edition O.S. Map of Hengistbury (Warren) Head, dates to 1809/11.

Mallett Photo.   The Priory Church and River Stour Christchurch   Christchurch